THE COMMONWEALTH AND INTERNATIONAL LIBRARY

Joint Chairmen of the Honorary Editorial Advisory Board

SIR ROBERT ROBINSON, O.M., F.R.S., LONDON

DEAN ATHELSTAN SPILHAUS, MINNESOTA

GEOGRAPHY DIVISION

General Editor: W. B. FISHER

An Agricultural Geography of Great Britain

26.2-73

An Agricultural Geography of Great Britain

by

D. W. GILCHRIST SHIRLAW

PERGAMON PRESS

OXFORD · NEW YORK · TORONTO
SYDNEY · BRAUNSCHWEIG

Pergamon Press Ltd., Headington Hill Hall, Oxford

Pergamon Press Inc., Maxwell House, Fairview Park, Elmsford,
New York 10523

Pergamon of Canada Ltd., 207 Queen's Quay West, Toronto 1

Pergamon Press (Aust.) Pty. Ltd., 19a Boundary Street,
Rushcutters Bay, N.S.W. 2011, Australia

Vieweg & Sohn GmbH, Burgplatz 1, Braunschweig

First edition 1966

Second revised impression (in metric units) 1971

Library of Congress Catalog Card No. 65–29069

Printed in Great Britain by Bell & Bain Ltd.

This book is sold subject to the condition
that it shall not, by way of trade, be lent,
resold, hired out, or otherwise disposed
of without the publisher's consent,
in any form of binding or cover
other than that in which
it is published.

08 016654 7 (flexicover)
08 016653 9 (hard cover)

CONTENTS

Contents

Section *IV* AGRICULTURAL REGIONS OF ENGLAND AND WALES

FOREWORD

IN THIS age of specialization, where the trend " to know more and more about less and less " continues, a study which attempts—and in my judgement achieves —a synthesis between the two subjects of agriculture and geography is an admirable counterbalance. Here is a book providing a wealth of knowledge of comprehensive range, yet of valuable factual condensation, which is most timely when planning of a regional character is being further developed. Let the reader but glance at the first paragraph of the author's introduction to Section I for an illustration of the availability of information necessary to a student of agricultural geography.

The author I know to be an inspired teacher of outstanding ability, thoroughly abreast of scientific research on his subject ; and who appeals still further to me as being as much at home in field and farm work as he is in the lecture room and research laboratory. Within these pages will be found recent historical developments which have led to an agricultural revolution (still proceeding) in the present century, together with up-to-date descriptions of soils, climate, topography, planning and farming systems. A most useful bibliography is provided at the end of each section. I warmly commend this lucid, informative and most readable book.

H. CECIL PAWSON

The University,
Newcastle upon Tyne

AUTHOR'S PREFACE

AGRICULTURE and geography are usually regarded as two separate studies; yet they are both branches of natural science and in many respects they are closely related. Thus the student of geography will sooner or later find himself considering matters essentially agricultural, such as various aspects of land utilization and the distribution of different soils. On the other hand, the student of agriculture will find that agricultural activities are controlled by such factors as relief, soil and climate—all aspects of physical geography.

In a sense, therefore, it is perhaps surprising that, though geography is usually considered an integral part of a general education, agriculture is not. In consequence, it is common for the geography student to consider agricultural topics quite divorced from their essential background of crop and animal husbandry. The corollary of this is that few textbooks on agriculture devote much of their space to the physical background of farming.

The present book in no way claims to be a textbook on either agriculture or geography. Rather it is an attempt to demonstrate the relationship between the two subjects, to provide a minimum agricultural background for the student of geography and, at the same time, a minimum geographical background for the student of agriculture. Emphasis has therefore been placed on the points of contact between these two subjects—soils, geology, climate, and systems of farming.

I wish to express my grateful thanks to Professor H. C. Pawson, who read the manuscript, made many helpful suggestions, and was kind enough to write the Foreword; to Professor W. B. Fisher, who greatly assisted me with the geographical data and who arranged for the publication of the book; to Mr. A. Main and Professor E. M. Carpenter, who supplied some most helpful information. I should also like to thank my colleague, Mr. A. A. Millar, on whose extensive knowledge of farming in Scotland I have been able to draw. My thanks are also due to Miss G. Gibson, who redrew my rought sketches, thus making them suitable for publication, and to Mrs. D. Grugan, who typed the original manuscript and retyped the various sections that I repeatedly altered.

SECTION I

Factors affecting the Choice of Farming Systems

INTRODUCTION

OF THE total area of the United Kingdom, which is about 24 million hectares some 80 per cent is devoted to agriculture. Of this only about a third can be considered as highly productive arable land; about 23 per cent is under permanent grass and about 28 per cent is very much less productive rough grazing. Despite an increasingly urban society, farming is still one of the major industries of the United Kingdom, and has the largest capital investment with an annual net output of over £1½ million, comparable with that of the motor-car industry. However, only about 4 per cent of the working population is engaged in agriculture, and therefore there are about 350,000 farmers of whom 300,000 are full-time. Over 80 per cent of the holdings are less than 40 hectares, though this figure varies somewhat from country to country; thus in Northern Ireland only 5·9 per cent of the holdings are over 40 hectares, whereas in England and Wales the figure is 21·7 per cent and in Scotland 21·9 per cent. In England and Wales the average-sized holding, excluding rough grazing, is 28 hectares, and in Northern Ireland only 12 hectares. Taken together, these figures serve to emphasize the importance of agriculture in the British economy and the preponderance of small units on which the industry is based.

Farming systems are many and diverse, each farmer adopting one that suits his particular circumstances. Nevertheless the choice of a farming system will be largely governed by the interaction of the following factors :

(a) Economic circumstances.
(b) Soil.
(c) Climate.
(d) Topography.
(e) The personal preference and individual skills of the farmer.
(f) The presence of disease.

It is important to remember that the farmer will most often choose to concentrate on those products that he feels will lead to the highest profit for his farm. This, in turn, depends on the efficient organization and deployment of the four factors of production : land, labour, capital, and individual skills of the farmer. Advice on planning a farming system, both for new entrants to the industry and for established farmers, is readily available through the National Agricultural Advisory Service and from the agricultural economics departments of the universities. Such advice will often lead to phenomenal improvements in the overall profitability of a farm.

CHAPTER 1

HISTORICAL SURVEY AND ECONOMIC FACTORS

THE economic factors controlling the choice of a farming system can be divided into two entities : (a) the law of demand and supply ; (b) the imposed economic climate resulting from government policy. For the most part these two act in unison, but at times they get out of step as, for example, when subsidies on a particular commodity lead to the production of that commodity in excess of the demand. On the other hand, local economic circumstances such as proximity to a market and the availability of labour, or even personal economic circumstances such as the availability of capital, may override the dictates of national economic policy, at least to a certain degree.

THE PERIOD BEFORE THE FIRST WORLD WAR

The effect of economic changes on the national farm over the last century is of particular interest. With the repeal of the Corn Laws in 1846, British agriculture was committed to facing free trade and especially competition from the developing countries. At first the effects of free trade were compensated by the steady growth of the industrial population and the lack of facilities for the transport of agricultural products from overseas. Indeed by 1872 agriculture had reached a peak of relative prosperity, which was never to be regained even to the present day. But by the end of the seventies the position had changed ; three years of bad weather culminated in 1879 with a disastrous summer when corn yields on many farms were reduced to 50 per cent of the normal ; for the first time, good harvests in North America and the importation of wheat meant that bad harvests at home were no longer to be compensated for by higher prices. The repeal of the Corn Laws was at last effective and thus began a decline in agricultural prosperity, which, except for a few brief years during and after the First World War, was to continue until 1937.

The decline in agricultural prices affected all types of goods. The introduction of refrigeration brought British livestock products into general competition with products from overseas, but the effect was less severe than with grain. The demand for cereals is less " elastic " than that for livestock products in that a falling price does not stimulate greater demand to take care of a surplus ; furthermore, in cereal growing the cost of production generally falls more slowly than the value of the product, largely because the major part of the costs are incurred at least twelve months before the product is sold ; again falling cereal prices mean cheaper food for livestock. In general, in a régime of falling prices arable crops are likely to be reduced and livestock production to be increased. This trend is illustrated in Figs. 1 and 2. Figure 1 traces the percentage distribution of the different classes of agricultural land between 1887 and 1962 ; Fig. 2 gives the numbers of dairy stock and the numbers of sheep over the same period.

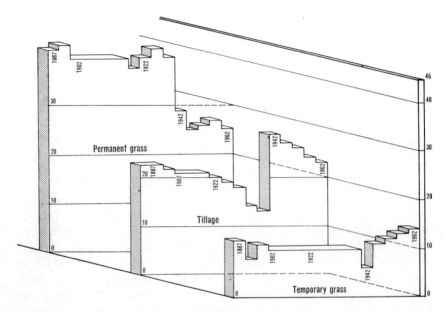

Fig. 1. Percentage distribution of different classes of agricultural land 1887–1962.

Between 1887 and 1937 the area of tillage dropped from 5 million to 3·4 million hectares; corn crops alone decreased by 1·2 million hectares. During the same period the total cattle population increased by 1·5 million.

THE FIRST WORLD WAR

This general trend was influenced to some extent by other factors. Thus, by the time of the First World War Britain had become dependent on imports for at least one-half of its food ; but it was not until the losses in shipping by enemy submarine activity in 1917 that it became obvious that positive measures would have to be taken to increase home food production. Already the war had brought higher prices and greater prosperity, but the Corn Production Act of 1917 gave the State power to order, through local executive committees, the ploughing out of grassland and other cultivation necessary to increase food production. At the same time the Act guaranteed farmers against a loss on wheat and oat crops. These measures led to some increase in arable land and by the end of the war about 1·2 million hectares of grass had been ploughed out.

THE INTER-WAR YEARS

The food situation in the latter half of the war meant that at the end of hostilities in 1918 the Government was full of good intentions to maintain home food production. In 1919 a Royal Commission recommended that the war-time

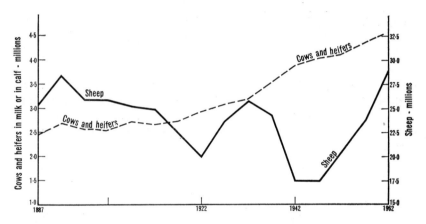

FIG. 2. Number of dairy stock and sheep stock 1887–1962.

emergency principle of guaranteeing prices for certain products should be continued. As a result in 1920 an Agriculture Act was passed which repealed the provisions of the 1917 Act and substituted arrangements whereby the farmer was guaranteed the theoretical cost of his crops. But the war-time boom in prices ended in 1920, and the fall in the price of wheat and oats was such that the farmers would probably have received £20 million under the 1920 Act. The Government refused to honour its signature and the Act was repealed in 1921. Farming had returned to its pre-war position. The first incursion into State control of agriculture was over. The trend of diminishing importance of arable farming and increasing livestock numbers was resumed.

By 1930 prices reached a record low and the position had become serious. Except for sugar beet, for which a subsidy was provided in 1925, it was not until

B

1931 that the first step, an Agricultural Marketing Act, was taken to help the British farmer. There followed a series of measures, including the Wheat Act of 1932, and by the outbreak of war in 1939 import quotas on many types of goods had been reimposed, and subsidies and grants on various classes of goods had been provided by the State. Yet these measures had not had time to take effect, and even between 1937 and 1939 the arable area fell by 59,000 hectares; in 1939 there were 1·0 million hectares less arable land than there had been in 1914. For the second time in twenty-five years British farmers were called upon to supply a major part of the nation's food. Maximum production with regard to economy in manpower became the dominating factor—economy in terms of money was of secondary importance.

THE SECOND WORLD WAR

As had happened in 1917, County War Agricultural Committees were responsible for the direction of agriculture in each county. Once again grassland was ploughed out and there was an increase in the area of *tillage* of 2·1 million hectares or about 44 per cent. The shortage of labour and the increased demand for meat led to a reduction of sheep numbers to the lowest level ever recorded over the period for which reliable records are available. On the other hand, the demand for milk, of special value for health during a war-time diet, meant that the rate of expansion of the national dairy herd, which was apparent prior to the First World War and during the inter-war years, was increased.

THE POST-WAR PERIOD

In the post-war period the Government was again determined that agriculture should not be allowed to become a forgotten industry. The war-time measures of security were largely embodied in the 1947 Agriculture Act though these were slightly modified by the 1957 Act. Under the provisions of these Acts an annual review is held in February by the Government and the National Farmers' Union of the economic conditions and prospects of the farming industry. At each review prices of the major farm products are fixed for the period immediately following the review. Furthermore, it is laid down that the price for any commodity must be at least 96 per cent of that fixed in the previous year; reductions in the guaranteed prices of livestock must not exceed 9 per cent in three successive years, and the total value of the guarantees and grants must not be less than 97·5 per cent of the total of the previous year. In this way stability has been brought to British agriculture, and the effects of this can be seen in Fig. 1. Moreover, by altering the emphasis on commodities the Government is able, at least to some extent, to control the type of farming that is followed by the nation's farmers.

It must not, however, be assumed that the changes in agriculture relating to the overall economic circumstances were uniform. Individual farmers meet economic crises in different ways. Farmers within easy reach of industrial centres have, for many years, concentrated on commodities for which there was a ready market. Thus even today, when transport is hardly a problem, there is a concentration of dairy farmers and market gardeners around our major cities ; often the conditions of soil and climate would suggest a different choice of enterprises. On the other hand, the advent of the Milk Marketing Board and more stringent regulations regarding milk production have brought the end of the true town dairy where cows were kept inside for the whole year round and fed on purchased hay and *concentrates*. But on the outskirts of the cities the " flying herds " remain, where cows are bought as soon as they calve and sold as soon as they are dry. These farmers have probably been least affected by the ebb and flow of the economic tide.

The average farmer is in no financial position to alter his system of farming at a moment's notice. If his farm is geared to the production of milk from grass, he will be unwilling to make a sudden change to corn growing. On the other hand, if he has recently spent thousands of pounds on modern machinery to handle corn, he will not readily contemplate a change to grass and milk production ; indeed he will probably be unable to obtain the capital so to do. It is for this sort of reason that changes in economic emphasis take time for their full effect to be seen, and it is this time lag between cause and effect that makes the task of those charged with planning the national farm more difficult. Moreover, if a farmer has changed his system of farming to meet the dictates of national economic policy, the State must accept some responsibility and ensure that his new system of farming gives him an adequate return over a number of years. During the Second World War many farmers changed from stock rearing to dairy production in areas where milk production would normally be considered marginal ; but milk production was heavily subsidized and would clearly repay the farmer who invested capital in new housing and milking equipment. After the war a significant drop in the price of liquid milk could have brought these farmers to the verge of bankruptcy. Yet to maintain the price of milk at a sufficiently high level to ensure an adequate return for the marginal farmers resulted in very high profits being obtained by efficient farmers in more favourable circumstances, and a consequent surplus of liquid milk.

CHAPTER 2

SOILS

OFTEN the choice of a farming system will be limited, or at least indicated, by particular soil conditions. Any natural soil can be considered to be the result of an interaction between five soil-forming factors : climate, geology or parent material, topography, vegetation, and time ; it will be seen that this list includes two of the factors already noted as controlling the choice of a farming system. Thus both climate and topography can affect this choice whether directly (see later), or through their influences on soil formation. When considering agricultural soils, it is clear that natural vegetation is often of little significance and that man's treatment of the land becomes an important soil-forming factor.

THE SOIL PROFILE

The description and classification of a soil is based on the soil profile characteristics, and a typical soil profile is illustrated in Fig. 3 ; a soil profile is seen either by taking advantage of ditches, road cuttings or quarries, or by digging a soil pit.

The different horizons are recognized by differences in one or more of the following properties : colour, texture, structure, or certain chemical properties. The horizons are grouped into A, B, C and D horizons, and where more than one horizon is recognized within the group they are distinguished by a subscript number. The A horizons are those that exhibit signs of the removal of organic or mineral material. In a climate where precipitation exceeds evaporation, i.e. where there is a predominant downward movement of water through soil profile, the A horizons are found at the top of the profile. Where horizons are present that represent the accumulation of organic material not mixed with the mineral material of the soil these are usually termed A_0 and A_{00} horizons ; the A_{00} horizon is the undecomposed litter layer and is sometimes termed an L horizon. The A_0 horizon is sometimes further divided into an F or fermentation layer and an H or humus layer. The A_1 horizon is the first horizon of the mineral soil and represents an admixture of organic and mineral material. The A_2 horizon usually shows signs of *leaching* of both organic material and the finer fractions of the soil ; it is paler in colour and is sometimes actually bleached grey or white. When examining a cultivated soil the A horizons will be found to be mixed together and the resultant cultivated horizon is called an S horizon. The S horizon may overlie the A_2 horizon or the B_1 horizon.

The B horizons are the horizons of deposition or illuviation. Generally at least two B horizons can be recognized and these are labelled B_1 and B_2. The B_1 horizon is often the zone of deposition of organic matter and the B_2 horizon is then the zone of deposition of mineral matter. The B horizons will often be of heavier texture than the A horizons as a result of the accumulation of clay. In some soils a *hard pan* may be found lying at the base of the A horizons.

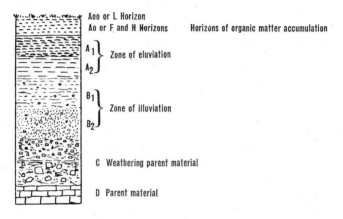

FIG. 3. Typical soil profile.

The C horizon is the weathered unconsolidated parent material which shows no accumulation either of organic material or of mineral matter. The D horizon is the parent rock. Transported soils are those where the soil material has been transported by ice, wind, water or gravity and in this case the underlying rock will have no relation to the soil. Some alluvial soils have been formed from relatively thin layers of deposits, and in this case the underlying unconsolidated material will have little relation to the soil ; this unconsolidated material is then termed a D horizon and the soil profile is an A, B, D type. With still other soils no B horizon exists and they are then A, C, D soils.

SOIL CLASSIFICATION

The concept that a particular soil is the result of the interaction of climate, geology, topography, vegetation, and time has led to a system of classification whereby soils are grouped into three main orders : (1) zonal, (2) intrazonal,

(3) azonal. The zonal soils are those whose characteristics are primarily determined by climate ; broadly their distribution follows climatic zones and the order is divided into sub-orders on this basis. Intrazonal soils are those where some factor other than climate has modified the soil characteristics ; thus intrazonal soils reflecting the character of the parent material, or the presence of salt, or the presence of poor drainage are found within the zonal belts ; the intrazonal order is further divided into calcimorphic, halomorphic and hydromorphic sub-orders. Azonal soils, for which there are no sub-orders, are those that possess no distinct profile characteristics, most often because they are young deposits (alluvia) or because they are situated in areas where erosion keeps pace with soil formation (skeletal soils or lithosols of mountain areas). A classification of world soils is given in Table 1 ; the Great Soil Groups of particular importance in the United Kingdom are italicized.

THE PODZOL

Podzols are mainly found to the north and west of a line running east across the country from Bristol to the south of the Pennines, then north along the Pennine Chain and finally demarcating the east coast of Scotland (see Fig. 4). These podzols are found either under coniferous forest or on heathland, particularly if the soil is sandy. Typically the podzol profile has the following horizons :

A_{00}. About 2·5 cm of litter (L horizon), consisting of almost undecomposed pine needles or residues of raw plant cover mixed possibly with peat.

A_0. This is a *mor humus* layer and is very acid, the litter having a low content of bases ; fungi are dominant in producing humus, and bacterial activity is at a minimum. Earthworms are practically absent and *pH values* of as low as 3·5 are common in both the F and H layers.

A_1. Dark-coloured mineral soil varying in thickness, and often absent in well-developed coniferous forest podzols.

A_2. Strongly leached and bleached layer. Podzols are formed in areas of high rainfall ; and the rainwater, already charged with carbon dioxide, picks up humus acids and probably other organic acids from the mor humus ; leaching with this acid solution dissolves the compounds normally responsible for the colour of the soil. Furthermore the mechanical leaching carries the finer fractions of the soil lower into the profile, leaving the coarser grained sand fractions behind. The A_2 horizon is thus a grey-white sandy layer. It is this horizon that gives the podzol its name, which is from the Russian and means " under ash ".

B_1. With heath podzols a hard pan about 0·3 cm thick will be found immediately below the bleached A_2 horizon ; this is a zone of maximum iron and possibly organic matter deposition. This pan is usually absent under coniferous forest. Below the pan, or below the A_2 horizon if no pan is present, is the zone

TABLE 1

A CLASSIFICATION OF THE GREAT SOIL GROUPS

Order	Sub-order	Great soil groups
Zonal soils	1. Soils of the cold zone	Tundra soils
	2. Light-coloured soils of arid regions	Desert soils Red Desert soils Sierozem Brown soils Reddish-brown soils
	3. Dark-coloured soils of semi-arid, subhumid, and humid grasslands	Chestnut soils Reddish Chestnut soils Chernozem soils Prairie soils Reddish Prairie soils
	4. Soils of the forest–grassland transition	Degraded Chernozem Non-calcic Brown or Shuntung Brown soils
	5. Light-coloured podzolized soils of the timbered regions	*Podzol soils* Grey wooded or Grey Podzolic soils *Brown Podzolic soils* *Grey-brown Podzolic soils* Red-yellow Podzolic soils
	6. Lateritic soils of forested warm-temperate and tropical regions	Reddish-brown Lateritic soils Yellowish-brown Lateritic soils Laterite soils
Intrazonal soils	1. Halomorphic (saline and alkali) soils of imperfectly drained arid regions and littoral deposits	Solonchak or Saline soils Solonetz soils Soloth soils
	2. Hydromorphic soils of marshes, swamps, seep areas, and flats	Humic-gley soils (includes Wiesenboden) Alpine meadow soils Bog soils Half-bog soils Low humic-gley soils Planosols Ground water Podzol soils Ground water Laterite soils
	3. Calcimorphic soils	*Brown Forest soils (Braunerde)* *Rendzina soils*
Azonal soils		*Lithosols* Regosols (includes dry sands) *Alluvial soils*

FIG. 4. Simplified soil map of Great Britain.

of deposition of organic matter sometimes referred to as the B_h horizon. Again the thickness of this horizon varies, but it is typically about 30 cm. It also varies in colour from black brown to light brown.

B_2. This is the zone of accumulation of iron and aluminium sesquioxides and of clay. It is therefore heavier in texture than the upper horizons and is typically rust coloured, though it may occur as a brown seam.

C. This is the weathered parent material and is variable in depth.

Many modifications to the profile described above may be found. Thus iron-deficient podzols occur in which the horizon of sesquioxides accumulation is absent. In other cases the ground water level is sufficiently high to give rise to a glei horizon : under waterlogged conditions the oxides of iron present give up their oxygen and the iron combines with sulphur originating from the decaying vegetation to give various compounds with a blue or green colour. Such an horizon is usually flecked with rust in old root channels where some oxidation can take place.

For the most part true podzols are of little agricultural importance since they occur in areas that are either too hilly or too swampy, or else the soil itself is too stony or too sandy. They are, however, of interest in forestry. Where heath podzols are being reclaimed for afforestation the first necessity is for deep ploughing, not only to bury the heather, but also to break up the pan and thus to give a more favourable habitat for tree growth. Deep ploughing will not prevent the heather from re-establishing itself ; consequently the young trees are encouraged to make rapid growth by the addition of fertilizers until they become the dominant species and convert the ploughed out heath podzol into a forest podzol. Some heath podzols can be reclaimed so that under good management they support improved grass swards. Such reclaimed land requires heavy applications of lime, phosphate, potash and nitrogen. With improved crop varieties it is even possible to cultivate some of this land for more varied cropping.

BROWN FOREST SOILS

Brown Forest soils, Grey-brown, and Brown Podzolic soils are found mainly to the south and east of the line defined above as demarcating the area of the podzols. They occur naturally under deciduous forest—the climax forest of much of Great Britain. The Brown Forest soils differ from the podzols in that the leaf fall from deciduous forest is much less resistant to bacterial breakdown than are the pine needles, and annually adds the equivalent of 2·5 tonnes per hectare of calcium carbonate to the soil. As a result the conditions are much less acid, soil population is much more abundant and the profile shows much less differentiation. In the soil classification given in Table 1, the Brown Forest soils appear as intrazonal soils on the basis that they are calcimorphic ; it may appear, however, that the dominant factor in their formation is vegetation and that this vegetation is largely dependent on climate ; certainly the deciduous forest is found in slightly warmer and drier conditions than the coniferous forest and it may thus be argued that the Brown Forest soils should be regarded as zonal soils. Synonyms of this class of soil include Brown Earths and Braunerde of Ramann.

A typical profile of a Brown Forest soil would be :

A_0. A thin litter horizon of undecomposed leaf fall (L horizon).

A_1. A deep layer of well-structured soil whose humus content decreases gradually with depth. The humus form is *mull* or mild ; the reaction is never below pH 4·5 and may be as high as pH 8·0. Earthworms and other soil animals are numerous and their activity prevents the development of well-defined F and H horizons ; mull humus appears to be characteristic of organic matter that has passed through the alimentary tract of soil animals. Bacterial decomposition is dominant. The colour of this horizon is described by the name Brown Earth.

B_1. The boundary between the A and B horizons is usually difficult to determine partly because of the gradual change from one to the other, and partly because the B horizon is not a true illuvial horizon but rather a layer built up by deep-reaching chemical weathering and oxidation of iron compounds. In some cases the B_1 horizon is heavier in texture than other horizons either as a result of it being an area of active clay synthesis or as a result of clay accumulation from mechanical eluviation from upper horizons. At times a clay horizon can be recognized as a separate B horizon.

C. In the true Brown Forest soil the B horizon merges gradually into the C horizon. The parent material is most likely to be basic in nature, and highly siliceous rocks are unfavourable for its development.

Natural Brown Forest soils under forest are rare in Great Britain ; for these soils were cleared of their tree cover many years ago and have been cultivated ever since. Most of the well-drained English soils may be assigned to this class. Just as there are all transitions between mull and mor humus, so there are all transitions between Brown Forest soils and podzols ; indeed the Brown Forest soil is sometimes regarded as an incipient podzol. The Brown Podzolic and the Grey-brown Podzolic soils are similar to Brown Forest soils, but are of lower base status and show a degree of podzolization. Most of the freely drained soils of Scotland and Wales may be assigned to these two classes.

Together the Brown Forest soils and the Grey-brown and Brown Podzolic soils dominate the intensive agriculture, not only of Great Britain, but also of much of Western and Central Europe and of the eastern and central United States of America. Indeed, Western civilization has grown up on these soils.

Depending on the degree of podzolization they are more or less acid in nature and poor in most plant nutrients, at least in an available form. After years of cultivation they may also become low in organic matter. Nevertheless, under good management and with adequate fertilizer applications the soils themselves present no real limitation to agriculture. The majority of research into soils, crops, and fertilizers has been conducted on these members of the Great Soil Groups. It is also interesting that more than one-half of the world's fertilizer is used on the Grey-brown Podzolic soils and their associates within Europe.

RENDZINAS

Rendzinas are found overlying chalk or limestone. Examples can be found on the North and South Downs, the Cotswolds, the Chiltern Hills, the Lincolnshire and Yorkshire Wolds, and the magnesian limestone belt running from North East England in a southerly direction to Nottingham. The rendzina is classified as an intrazonal calcimorphic soil, and a typical profile would be as follows :

A_0. A thin layer of plant debris from the natural vegetation (often of sheep's fescue and agrostis grasses).

A_1. A black or dark grey mineral soil with a high organic matter content ; the colour depends on the relative abundance of mineral particles and of organic matter. The dark colour is the result of the formation of chalk *humates*. The A_1 horizon is typically about 12 cm in depth and usually contains some stone; however, it may be as deep as 50 cm. The reaction is around neutrality; soil animals such as earthworms which contribute to a marked uniformity in the horizon are abundant.

C. Directly below the A_1 horizon lies the weathering parent material ; no B horizon can be recognized, though in some profiles an accumulation of precipitated calcium carbonate below the A horizon may lead to the recognition of a Ca horizon.

Rendzinas may vary in texture from light sandy loams to loams. Their main limitation for agricultural use lies in the thinness of the A horizons ; thus it is seldom possible to plough more than 15 cm deep, and where this is the case farming is restricted to shallow-rooted crops. Indeed much of the chalk lands is typically fescue dominant grassland, stocked mainly with sheep. Deeper soils have given sheep and barley land : a system of farming whereby sheep build up the fertility of the soil which is cashed by the farmer through a barley crop.

HYDROMORPHIC SOILS

Two types of hydromorphic soils (intrazonal soils formed under the dominant influence of water) occur in Great Britain : hill or acid peat and Fen or basin peat. All peats are the result of the accumulation of organic matter under waterlogged conditions ; the essential difference between the two types is that acid peat is formed in areas of high rainfall, whereas basin peat is the result of excessive ground water. Rainfall, charged as it is with carbon dioxide, is acidic and in leaching through the layers of organic matter maintains acidic conditions. Ground water, on the other hand, has a generally high mineral content and, though the anaerobic conditions lead to the accumulation of organic matter, the peat so formed is much less acid and much richer in nutrients.

Acid peats are found extensively in upland areas, e.g. the Highlands of Scotland, Ireland, the Lake District, Wales and the Pennine Chain. The profiles may vary considerably depending partly on the vegetation and partly on the depth of peat overlying the mineral strata. This overburden of peat may be regarded as an A_0 horizon. Where a number of distinctive layers of peat are present the top one may be termed A_0 and the remainder as successive D horizons. Acid peat moors are of limited agricultural value, but they may be of some economic significance either for fuel, horticultural peats, or as grouse moors.

Reclamation of acid peats depends partly on the depth of peat and partly on the degree of admixture of mineral material ; often acid peats occur in bleak and unfavourable climatic conditions. Nevertheless extensive areas of acid peat land have been reclaimed in Scotland ; generally the objective has been to establish good grass *swards* for grazing and hay and pioneer crops are taken to prepare the land to this end. Drainage is the first essential and this is often accomplished by deep open ditches. When the land has dried out sufficiently it is usually ploughed deeply and then extensively cultivated to obtain a seed bed. This process may take a number of years. Many applications of lime will be required followed by dressings of phosphate, potash and even nitrogen. In some cases the land may be directly reseeded to grass, but in others pioneer crops of rape, turnips, or potatoes may be taken.

The most extensive area of basin peat in Great Britain is in the Fenlands of Yorkshire, Lincolnshire, and Norfolk. The profile of the Fen soils is essentially similar to that of the acid peats, with the exception that the peat layer is often found to lie on heavily *gleyed* mineral horizons. Following reclamation these soils can be highly fertile and impose few restrictions on agriculture. The land must first be dried by the construction of drainage works : frequently the land lies below sea level and pumping stations will be required. It is often desirable to *marl* the land or possibly to spread sand on it before ploughing. Heavy applications of fertilizer including lime are always required, though good crops are grown after the initial reclamation. Applications of the trace element copper may be necessary to prevent the occurrence of reclamation disease.

AZONAL SOILS

Lithosols are skeletal soils found in the uplands. Generally they occur in areas where soil erosion keeps pace with soil formation, and virtually no soil profile exists. They are of little significance to agriculture except for hill sheep. The other class of azonal soils is the alluvial soils. These are comparatively young deposits and again show little signs of profile development. In contrast to the lithosols, however, they are often prized for crop production ; they are usually sandy loams, well drained and easily cultivated. Whilst not necessarily inherently fertile so far as plant nutrients are concerned, such soils will respond well to applications of farmyard manure and artificial fertilizers. Limitations for agriculture will result where the land is sufficiently low lying to be liable to flooding ; in such cases their best utilization may be as grassland. Otherwise they will carry a wide range of crops and will support high yields under good management.

CHAPTER 3

CLIMATE AND TOPOGRAPHY

CLIMATE can affect the choice of a farming system either indirectly through its influence on soil formation, or directly through such factors as the length of the growing season, the occurrence of frost and the availability of water for crop growth. An examination of a world map of climates shows that Great Britain lies in a cool temperate zone except for the extreme north of Scotland, which lies in a cold temperate zone. But the climate is so much affected by the proximity of the Atlantic Ocean, and particularly by the warming current of the Gulf Stream, that it can in a general way be regarded as maritime. Within this general classification a number of somewhat ill-defined climatic regions may be recognized (Fig. 5). Thus the western half of the country has a warmer winter and is very much wetter throughout the year than the eastern half; the coldest winter is experienced in East Anglia. Furthermore, the western half has a generally cooler summer than the eastern half, but the greatest differentiation in the summer temperature is from north to south and the highest mean summer temperatures are found in the south east. In all cases the coastal strip has climates which are modified by the sea.

These differences in climate lead to interesting broad differences in systems of farming. Thus East Anglia, with its cold dry winter and hot dry summer has earned the title of the " grain farm of Great Britain " and it is only here that bread wheats of comparable quality to imported wheats can be grown : quality in bread wheats and in malting barley is dependent on warm dry conditions before harvest. On the western side of the country oats is the dominant cereal because it can best withstand, and indeed prefers, a cool moist climate. The western half of the country, with its warm wet winters and comparatively cool wet summers, is better suited to the production of grass to be utilized by beef or by dairy cattle. It is for this reason that Devon has been the birthplace of two of our breeds of cattle—the North Devon beef breed and the South Devon *dual purpose* breed ; Devonshire cream is famous throughout the country. Herefordshire is renowned throughout the world for its fattening pastures, which led to the development of the Hereford beef breed, members of which have been exported over many years and have been the foundation stock of range cattle in many countries. The names of Cheshire and Lancashire are always associated with dairy pastures

[1] This is less true today with an increased emphasis on barley for livestock production and the development of new varieties of barley.

and the production of cheeses, whereas Cumberland and Westmorland are to this day the home of the northern Dairy Shorthorn. Farther north still is the home of the Ayrshire dairy cattle, until a few years ago one of our most numerous

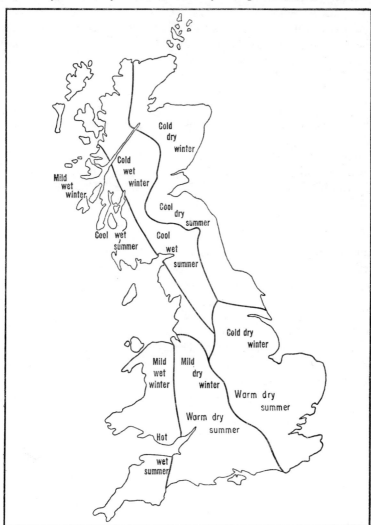

Fig. 5. Climatic regions of Great Britain.

breeds. Galloway has given its name to one of the hardiest of the beef breeds, and the Western Highlands to yet another. In each case these developments have resulted from the favourable climate for the production of grass. The grassland research station is at Hurley near Maidenhead, but many of our best strains of grasses have been developed at Aberystwyth. On the other hand, cereal varieties have mainly been developed in the eastern side of the country, and the N.I.A.B. centre for cereal trials is at Cambridge.

Altitude has a similar effect on climate as latitude. Thus for every 200 metres increase in altitude the mean temperature falls by 1°C, in consequence the growing season (i.e. the period during which the soil temperature exceeds 6°C) is shortened by about six days. For any region there is a limiting height above which crops will fail to make satisfactory growth; 200 metres is regarded as critical for general farming in the British Isles, with a growing season of about one month shorter than the surrounding districts at sea level. However, wheat can be ripened up to 300 metres and oats and barley up to 475 metres. It is for this reason (together with the before-mentioned fact that oats can best withstand wet conditions) that oats have been until recently the dominant cereal in the western half of the country and in hilly areas such as Wales, the Lake District and the Scottish Highlands.

On the other hand, altitude has an advantage for the production of seed potatoes. This is because aphids, which carry and spread virus diseases, are less numerous above 140 metres. At one time almost all commercial potato seed production in England and Wales was above this level. However, modern techniques of *systemic insecticides* have enabled this specialist branch of farming to be carried on at lower altitudes.

Local differences in climate can have very striking effects. Thus low land surrounded by higher ground will usually form a frost pocket. By radiation of heat after sunset the soil and the air immediately above it are cooled. Cold air is more dense than warm air and will flow downhill, collecting at the bottom of the slope; this effect will be most noticeable on a clear calm night when a temperature difference of up to 5°C can be observed between the high-lying and the low-lying ground; a crop on low-lying ground may suffer from frost damage, whereas a similar crop on higher-lying ground may not. This effect can be sufficiently serious to rule out certain crops such as early potatoes and especially horticultural crops.

The slope of the land can have a striking effect; thus in many valleys running east–west, the north side will receive a much more concentrated insolation than the south side. This may have affected soil formation by its influence on vegetation. Certainly the effect on present farming can be dramatic.

Shelter belts may also give rise to local differences in climates. A dense shelter belt gives the greatest reduction in wind force, but this is limited to a distance from the belt of about 20 times its height. A less dense belt will give some shelter to a distance up to 30 times its height. The dense belt is therefore more suitable for sheltering stock and the less dense belt is more suitable for sheltering crops.

TOPOGRAPHY

The influence of topography through its effect on soils and climate has already been discussed, but topographical limitations can directly control the choice of a farming system. Thus a slope may be sufficiently steep to prevent ploughing even with modern equipment, or at least make it so hazardous or so uneconomic as to be out of the question. In such cases the only possible utilization may be as grassland. Where the topographical limitation is not so severe ploughing may be possible, but not combine harvesting ; in this case it may be desirable to plough out the old pasture and reseed it to increase productivity. In still other cases crops other than cereals may be considered possible. At the other extreme land may be so flat as to be marshy and may then develop a lacustrine peat. When this occurs in a small area the cost of drainage works may not be justified.

The land itself may be well suited for arable cropping, but it may be rendered inaccessible to modern farm machinery ; this may be the case with alluvial soils near the river which are cut off from the main farm by a second flood water bank. The better pastures of *in-bye* land on hill farms may be regarded as a topographical influence inasmuch as they are the result of their proximity to the steading ; such pastures are more intensively grazed and receive in consequence a greater proportion of the droppings of livestock. A similar situation can develop on large lowland farms carrying both dairy and arable enterprises ; the fields farthest from the buildings are often of much lower fertility than those near the buildings. In many cases two rotations may be practised : one around the buildings, based on alternate husbandry with the ley as the pivot of the rotation ; and the other on the outlying land, based mainly on cash cropping. A similar situation may develop if some of the fields are cut off from the main farm by a major road.

C

CHAPTER 4

THE PERSONAL PREFERENCE
OF THE FARMER

So FAR factors largely outside the influence of the farmer have been considered for their effect on the choice of a system of farming. Whilst it is clear that these factors must in most cases dominate the choice, the personal preference of the farmer will influence the system in many ways. One of the most obvious ways in which the farmer's preference operates is in the choice of breeds of stock, and the choice of a breed may affect the farming system. Thus a farmer in a predominantly dairying area who elects to keep Jerseys will follow a slightly different cropping system to one who keeps Friesians. There are two major reasons for this :

(a) Jersey milk with an average fat content of over 5 per cent is subject to a quality premium. This means that the farmer receives more per litre than he would for Friesian milk (which has a fat content of only about 3·5 per cent) and can, in consequence, afford to spend more on food-stuffs per litre of milk produced.

(b) The Jersey is a much smaller animal than the Friesian, and high-yielding Jerseys require a more concentrated diet.

Together these two factors mean that less reliance will be placed on roughages such as silage and hay, and probably on home-grown cereals ; more emphasis will be placed on purchased concentrated feeds. This will be reflected in the farming system either by carrying a greater number of stock or by devoting more of the land to cash crops.

A similar effect may result from the choice of breed on a predominantly beef breeding farm. Some breeds such as the Angus require better conditions than others such as the Galloway. The choice of breed in this case may force the farmer to use his land more intensively than his neighbours. Similar situations attend the choice of a sheep breed or the selection of crossbred sheep.

In many cases this choice will extend further than just the selection of a particular breed. Farmers in grassland areas may elect to become dairy farmers or beef farmers ; in either case they can decide whether or not to have a sub-sidiary enterprise of sheep. Further they will decide whether to manage their land intensively with a major investment in fertilizers, or extensively with a major investment in feeding stuffs. The objective of a farmer is generally to make money, often as much as possible, but with a good farmer this objective will always be kept within the limits set by the demands of good husbandry. On the other hand, the farmer may not keep the livestock, or grow the crops which would give him the highest monetary return, because he gains more satisfaction from other enterprises ; again he may be prepared to accept a lower return from less intensive farming in return for an easier life than he would have were he farming intensively.

This freedom of choice of the farmer may well be the dominant factor in determining the system of farming on a particular farm ; certainly it makes difficult generalizations regarding systems of farming in different districts. Furthermore, modern developments in machinery, in weed control, in fertilizers, and in crop varieties have combined to make possible a far greater choice of farming system on less-favoured farms ; a wide choice has always been possible on well-favoured land.

THE PRESENCE OF DISEASE AND PESTS

The production of seed potatoes at higher altitudes to avoid virus infections from aphids has already been mentioned. But there are other diseases which may impose limitations on cropping. Under too frequent potato growing, potato root eelworm is liable to become a pest ; the only sure way of combating this pest is to avoid growing potatoes for at least six years. The presence of potato root eelworm could therefore impose a severe limitation on cropping. This situation has developed in some of the more important potato growing areas such as in certain areas of the Fens.

The disease Take-all in wheat, caused by a soil-borne fungus *Ophiobolus*, results from too frequent cropping with wheat. Again the only cure is to avoid growing wheat for a number of years, and this could be a serious limitation. Clover sickness is yet another example of a similar disease.

In the case of certain livestock diseases a slaughter policy is in force. Compared with crop diseases the results are usually more dramatic and receive greater publicity, but they are not so long lasting. Thus an outbreak of foot and mouth disease leads to the slaughter of all cloven hoofed animals on the farm, and restocking cannot take place for a minimum of six months. For the stock farmer this may be thought to impose a severe limitation on his farming ; but, provided he intends to restock at the end of the prohibition order, it will in the event have very little effect on his farming system ; if the outbreak has occurred in the early spring it may lead to the farmer devoting a greater acreage to cash crops, but he may still require much of his grassland for conservation for winter keep.

BIBLIOGRAPHY

BRADE-BIRKS, S. GRAHAM. *Good Soil*, Teach Yourself Farming Series. E.U.P. (1959).

COPPOCK, J. T. *An Agricultural Atlas of England and Wales.* Faber and Faber Ltd (1964).

DEPARTMENT OF AGRICULTURE FOR SCOTLAND. *Farm Management Handbook.* H.M.S.O. (1959).

DEXTER, K. and BARBER, D. *Farming for Profits.* Penguin (1961).

FRANKLIN, T. B. *A History of Agriculture.* Bell (1948).

GRESSWELL, R. KAY. *The Weather and Climate of the British Isles.* Hulton (1961).

JACKS, G. V. *Soil.* Nelson (1954).

MINISTRY OF AGRICULTURE, FISHERIES AND FOOD. *The Farm as a Business,* Revised Series. H.M.S.O. (1963).

MURRAY, Sir K. A. H. *Agriculture (History of the Second World War).* H.M.S.O. and Longmans, Green (1955).

ORWIN, C. S. *A History of English Farming.* Nelson (1949).

RUSSELL, Sir E. J. *The World of the Soil.* Collins (1957).

THE AGRICULTURAL BRANCH OF THE METEOROLOGICAL OFFICE (AIR MINISTRY). *Weather and the Land.* Bulletin No. 165, Ministry of Agriculture, Fisheries and Food. H.M.S.O. (1955).

WHETMAN, E. H. *British Farming 1939–49.* Nelson (1952).

WHYTE, R. O. *Crop Production and Environment.* Faber & Faber (1960).

The Farming Systems of Great Britain

INTRODUCTION

THE farming systems of Great Britain may be classified in a number of ways; the following divisions are based on the type of product:

(a) Hill sheep farming and hill sheep with cattle.
(b) Dominantly stock rearing.
(c) Stock rearing and fattening.
(d) Dairy farming.
(e) Mixed dairying and stock rearing, often with hill sheep.
(f) Mixed dairying and arable.
(g) Mixed dairying and fattening, usually with some arable.
(h) Mixed fattening and arable.
(i) Dominantly arable.
(j) Horticulture and market gardening, often with some livestock.
(k) Pigs and poultry.

Within each of these systems there are many variations. Thus the " mixed dairying and arable farms " include those where dairying is dominant and those where the arable enterprise is the more important. In the same way " mixed fattening and arable farms " include the following: (i) those based largely on wheat and cattle; (ii) those based mainly on arable farming but with significant livestock enterprises; (iii) the traditional corn and sheep farms; (iv) corn and sheep farms where there are other cash crops.

CHAPTER 1

HILL SHEEP FARMING
AND HILL SHEEP WITH CATTLE

THERE are about 6·5 million hectares of rough hill grazing in Great Britain; of this total over 4·5 million hectares are in Scotland, nearly a million are in Wales and a further 0·2 million are in Cumberland and Westmorland. These areas, together with the Cheviots and the Pennines in the north, are those with the greatest density of hill sheep farms. Many of these areas, and indeed districts within the areas, have developed their own breeds of mountain sheep; some of these breeds such as the Herdwick and the Derbyshire Gritstone are very localized, whereas others such as the Scottish Blackface and the Cheviot are widespread. In some of the more important breeds distinctive strains have been developed; thus the North Country Cheviot, found mainly in the north of Scotland, is a larger animal than the Cheviot and is recognized as a separate breed; again there are two distinct types of Scottish Blackface—the Lanark type and the finer boned, lighter fleeced, Newton Stewart type. A map showing the distribution of the mountain breeds of sheep is given in Fig. 6.

It was not until the end of the eighteenth century that extensive sheep farming was introduced to the Highlands of Scotland. Accent was then on the production of wether sheep with breeding stock only on the lowest-lying and most-sheltered *hirsels*. It may be argued that this was at the time the most productive use that could be made of the Highlands, since much of them are too exposed for breeding ewes. However, the introduction of refrigeration and consequent importation of frozen lamb from abroad, combined with a change in consumer taste, led to a reduction in the profitability of wether lambs and today there is no secure market for this product. As a result more breeding ewes are now left on higher hirsels than before and the highest hirsels have been abandoned.

Today the major products of the hill farms are as follows:

(a) *Wether sheep*. These are mainly store lambs, but some are sold fat from the better hills.

(b) *Cast ewes*. These are sold at five or six years old for crossing at lower levels with the Border Leicester ram and the production of cross-bred ewe lambs.

31

(c) *Wool.* The clip of a hill ewe is usually 1·8–2·3 kilos. On a flock of 400 ewes this will net about £300 and makes a major contribution to the gross output.

(d) *Ewe (female breeding) lambs.* Generally the lambing percentage of a hill flock will be about 80 per cent. Thus for every 100 ewes about 40 ewe lambs per year will be born. If the ewes are kept for four lamb crops about 25 per cent of them will be replaced annually. From 100 ewes, therefore, only about 15 ewe lambs, usually the poorer ones, will be sold. In a poor lambing year, after a bad winter, this number will be even smaller ; in some years, all the ewe lambs will be required for replacements.

At the time of writing ewes on a true hill farm will on the average leave an annual profit (including subsidies) of about £2 per head. Of the total output about 45 per cent will be from the sale of wether lambs, about 25 per cent from the sale of gimmer lambs, about 15 per cent from the sale of draft or cast ewes, and a further 15 per cent from the sale of wool. These figures will vary from farm to farm and from season to season, but it can be estimated that, to yield a reasonable living for a man and his family, a hill farm should be large enough to carry at least 400 breeding ewes and preferably some breeding cattle.

All areas of hill sheep farming have much in common. In the Highlands the farms usually consist of a small area of in-bye land with 400 hectares or more of rough grazings. On the Pennines, in the Border Country, and in the Lake District many of the hills are common grazings, and the flocks of several farmers graze together on the same ground. On the better hills the stocking rate will be one ewe to between 1 and 2 hectares; on the poorer hills 4 or even 5 hectares may be required. The natural vegetation consists of heather, bilberry, coarse grasses such as flying bent (*Molinia*), moor mat grass (*Nardus*), hair grasses (*Aira*), sheep's fescue (*Festuca*) and bent (*Agrostis*), and sedges such as draw moss. In Wales the conditions are somewhat different : many of the mountains are bare and rocky though others are covered by grasses ; there is very little heather. The proportion of cultivated land to hill grazings is higher than in Scotland or on the Pennines, but the majority of the sheep must be brought off the hill in the winter, and the limit to stocking density is often fixed by the availability of lowland winter keep.

THE SHEPHERD'S YEAR ON THE HILL FARM

On some hill farms the ewe hoggs are sent to lower land sometime in October for their first winter. By this time the wether lambs, the ewe lambs not required for breeding, and the cast ewes will have been sold ; any new rams required for the season's mating will have been purchased. With a pure-bred flock, rams are invariably bought in at regular intervals to prevent in-breeding. The months of October and November are a period of recuperation for the ewe before she is mated again. Tupping usually commences at the end of November, the 28th being the classical date. If the ewes were mated earlier than this, lambing would

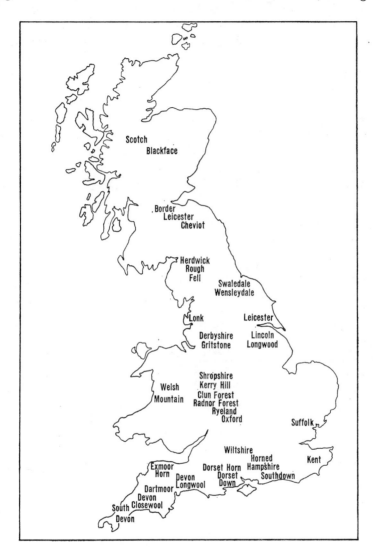

Fig. 6. Origin of breeds of sheep.

commence before the winter was over and in conditions which would lead to a high mortality in both ewes and lambs ; later mating would not allow sufficien time for the lambs to grow before the onset of the next winter. On some farms mating will take place on in-bye land, if sufficient is available ; this practice may lead to a higher lambing percentage since the ewes are in a better condition at mating and there is more certainty that they will be served by the ram. The ewes are in-lamb on the hill between December and April. In most areas supplementary feeding will only be given during severe snow storms. It is argued that this practice keeps the ewes from becoming dependent on hand feeding and maintains the hardiness of the breed. Some hill farmers, however, particularly in the north of England and in Aberdeenshire, feed hay regularly throughout the winter. Lambing takes place towards the end of April, sufficiently early to take advantage of the spring growth on the hills. The flock may at this time be again brought onto the in-bye land, though a large number of ewes are lambed on the hill. After lambing, the ewes return to the hill until June when the male lambs are castrated and the geld ewes (i.e. those that have not borne a lamb) are clipped. The milk ewes are clipped in July. In August the sheep are dipped and the lambs weaned. The sale of wether lambs, surplus ewe lambs, and cast ewes begins about this time.

CATTLE ON THE HILL FARM

It is often argued that hill sheep farming is more profitable if it is combined with a cattle enterprise. The cattle can graze rough pasture that is not suited to sheep and, to a degree at least, they can control bracken. Thus cattle grazing can lead to pasture improvement and to a consequent increase in the overall stocking-rate. On the other hand, the cattle may compete with the sheep for the in-bye land at tupping time and during lambing.

Hill cattle will usually belong to one of the following breeds : Galloway, Highland, and Welsh Black. They may be kept pure or they may be crossed with either the Shorthorn or with the Hereford. The system of management is generally to mate the cow in June or July so that she will calve in March or April. During the winter the cows will receive supplementary feed and many of them are wintered indoors in yards or in byres. The calves are born outdoors and run with their dams throughout the summer. They are weaned in October and usually sold at suckler sales held in the late autumn. The return from such a system can be expected to be about £20 per cow per year. On the basis that one cow will require as much land as five ewes it may appear that hill cattle are more productive than hill sheep. But hill sheep make use of land that cattle cannot graze and a fairer comparison would be with upland sheep. The upland sheep is a larger and heavier type and will leave a margin of about £4 per head. There is, therefore, little difference in the relative profitabilities of the two enterprises and, if it was merely a case of replacing five ewes with one cow, little advantage would be gained. However, cattle and sheep are to some extent complementary and an increase in cattle numbers does not bring a proportional decrease in sheep numbers. It is for this reason that hill farms with both sheep and cattle enterprises are more profitable than those with sheep alone.

FORESTRY

One further point should be considered in relation to hill farming, and that is the development of forestry. At the present time forests and woodland cover 1·5 million hectares of the rough land in Great Britain and this area is continually increasing. The demands of the hill sheep farmer and those of the forester often clash since they both want to have the best land. Extensive planting brings with it social disturbances and consequent problems which are at least numerous if not insuperable. New villages are often required to house the forestry workers and it is not always easy to attract workers to these villages, which are mostly remote and have few facilities. For many years the demand of the country workers for a higher standard of living, not only from the point of view of monetary rewards, but also from the point of view of a fair share of the social services, has led to the drift of workers from the country to the town. The increased demand for labour by the Forestry Commission has done little to stem this flow. Furthermore, many of the workers who have been attracted from the towns are unable to adjust themselves to rural life.

The present trend of an increase in the size of hill farms brought about by existing occupiers buying up neighbouring farms as they come on to the market can be expected to continue. The combination of larger cattle and sheep rearing farms together with forestry may provide the answer to many of the difficulties of finding the best utilization of this part of the national farm.

CHAPTER 2

DOMINANTLY STOCK REARING FARMS

THESE farms are found in the upland areas rather than on the true hills. They are widely distributed along the more accessible glens in the Highlands, in the north east of Scotland, in Orkney, in the Border Country, on the foot hills of the Pennines, in Wales and in the Lake District. Included in this group there is a wide range in the size of holdings from the part-time West Highland croft, which is usually a stock rearing holding with two or three cattle, a dozen sheep and a few hens, to the large-scale stock rearing farms with two hundred or more cattle and perhaps two thousand head of sheep. With such a range it is difficult to describe a typical holding and the term average can have little meaning. The sort of farm which would be included in this group is one with a homestead in the valley together with a few fields of crop and grass ; there would be a variable but usually large area on the high ground, part or all of which may be common grazing. About two-thirds of the low-lying land will be permanent grass and two-thirds of the remainder will be under fodder crops such as oats, roots and kale. The majority of these farms are found on marginal land—so described because the land will only repay cropping when prices are high.

CATTLE ON DOMINANTLY STOCK REARING FARMS

The two main sources of income from these farms are cattle and sheep, though many have a subsidiary enterprise of poultry. Cattle may account for 25 per cent of the gross output and sheep for about 50 per cent. Some cattle are kept in single suckling herds as described for the hill farms, but calving is often earlier and on the most-favoured land will take place from Christmas. A modification to the system is multiple suckling where calves are brought in at a few days old and nurse cows are kept. The nurse cow will often be a *dual purpose* animal capable of giving an annual milk yield of about 3000 litres; she may have been *culled* from the dairy herd either because she lost a quarter or was a slow milker ; a good cow can be expected to rear up to nine calves : in the early stages of her lactation she will suckle four calves for about three months—these are then weaned and a further three calves are suckled and finally two ; on the average six or seven calves will be reared. The calves on this system will be either dairy heifers or cross-bred calves from the dairy herd.

Thus from marginal farms the cattle sales may be any of the following :

(a) Store cattle suitable for fattening at a young age and being pure-bred Hereford, Aberdeen Angus, Beef Shorthorn or Welsh Black, or crosses between these breeds. Many of these are single suckled.

(b) Store cattle suitable for fattening at an intermediate age and being crosses between dairy cows and beef breeds, or between white Shorthorn bulls and Galloway cows (the Blue-grey), or pure Friesian stirks.

(c) Dairy heifers that have been reared on multiple-suckling and are often sold as new calvers.

SHEEP ON DOMINANTLY STOCK REARING FARMS

As previously mentioned, the cast ewes from the hill flocks are sold to lower-lying farms. The cast hill ewe is still capable of breeding and indeed, under the

TABLE 2

TYPICAL LONGWOOL–MOUNTAIN BREED CROSSES

Longwool breed	Mountain breed	Name of cross
Border Leicester	Scottish Blackface	Mule or Greyface
Border Leicester	Cheviot	Half-bred
Border Leicester	Swaledale	Swale mule
Border Leicester	Welsh Mountain	Welsh Half-bred
Wensleydale	Swaledale	Masham
Teeswater	Swaledale	Masham

less rigorous conditions of the marginal farm, she will rear a bigger lamb. She is therefore mated to a ram of one of the longwool breeds : Border Leicester, Wensleydale or Teeswater. The longwool breeds are larger in frame, earlier maturing, deeper milking, and of higher fecundity than the mountain breeds and it is these qualities which it is hoped will be passed on to the offspring. Typical longwool–mountain breed crosses are listed in Table 2.

About 10 per cent of the males from such a cross are sold fat off the ewe. The rest of the wethers may be fattened on roots and then sold fat or they may be sold as store lambs for fattening on still lower lying farms. The ewe lambs are sold for crossing with a down breed, again on more favoured land. The cross between the longwool and the mountain breed represents the second stage in what is known as stratification of types in sheep breeding, the first stage being the pure-bred flocks on the hills.

There are many variations to the system of stratification here described. Thus on some of the better marginal land a down ram, especially the Suffolk, may be used instead of the longwool. In this case a higher percentage of the wether lambs will be sold fat off the ewe and less than 50 per cent may have to be root-fed. The ewe lambs may be either sold fat, or sold as cross-bred ewes for subsequent crossing with another down breed. In other cases a cross-bred ram (possibly Border Leicester × Suffolk) may be used, but this is moving away from an organized system of cross-breeding. It is interesting that similar systems of stratification are found in other areas of the world. Thus in Australia the cull Merino ewe from the back-country is taken to the wheat belt and there crossed with the Romney Marsh, Border Leicester, or Dorset Horn ; the female progeny are sold to the irrigated areas to be crossed with Southdown rams.

The output of sheep from these flocks may comprise the following :

(a) Fat wether lambs.
(b) Wether lambs for mutton.
(c) Ewe lambs for breeding.
(d) Draft ewes for mutton.

In average conditions a profit of about £4 per ewe could be expected. The total output per hectare (not including fell grazing) could be expected to be about £50 of which £25 will be derived from sheep, £12·5 from cattle, and £12·5 from other enterprises. The margin per hectare at the time of writing could be expected to be about £17.

CROPPING ON THE MARGINAL FARM

The cropping of the in-bye land will be mainly directed towards providing winter keep for the cattle; with intensive multiple-suckling herds almost 0·3 hectare of grass and fodder crops per cow will be required. With single-suckling herds 0·8 hectare will be necessary. Grassland will be required for grazing and for conservation for winter feed either as hay or, less often, as silage. The cereal most often grown is oats since it withstands the conditions better than barley. Root crops are extensively grown, especially in Scotland, though today there is a tendency to grow more grass for silage and to grow less roots. Some of the Scottish upland farmers have a subsidiary enterprise of seed potatoes.

CHAPTER 3

STOCK REARING AND FATTENING FARMS

STOCK rearing and fattening farms are located at somewhat lower elevations than dominantly stock rearing farms, where both soil and climatic conditions are well suited to the cultivation of fodder crops, but not so well suited to the widespread cultivation of cash crops such as potatoes, wheat and sugar beet. Such conditions are found particularly in the north east of Scotland in Aberdeenshire and in Orkney, in the uplands of the south east and east of Scotland, in belts along the lower slopes of the Pennines, in the Cleveland and Cambrian upland systems, including Anglesey and the Lleyn peninsula, and in North Devon.

In some respects these farms have much in common with the stock rearing farms previously discussed. The cropping programmes are very similar except that in many cases more turnips and swedes will be grown. Sheep are generally of less relative importance than in the previous system though the density of stocking will be greater as a result of the overall higher productivity. Of the gross output 50 per cent may be from cattle and only 30 per cent from sheep—the remainder being from subsidiary enterprises.

CATTLE ON STOCK REARING AND FATTENING FARMS

Most of the beef calves are cross-bred and multiple-suckled, but two other systems should be mentioned. Firstly, the production of early beef from single-suckled herds is a fairly recent development which may well prove to be successful; if the calf is born in January and kept on a moderately high plane of nutrition it will be ready for sale as early beef during the following year in the high-priced period of February and March. Secondly, the system of rearing bought calves on the bucket and carrying them through to beef has become more popular since the introduction of early weaning.

The beef cattle may be summer or winter fattened and the output from any one farm may be dominantly one or the other. Single-suckled calves will be either sold as early beef at 12–14 months of age or as more mature beef at just over two years of age. In both cases they will probably be wintered in yards or courts, though in sheltered districts some may be outwintered; they are usually turned out in April and receive turnips or swedes as supplementary feed until the grass grows; the majority will be fat by the August of their second year. The cattle that are to be fattened during the winter will again be wintered in

39

yards, but some of them may be tied in byres for their last two months. When they are almost ready for the butcher they will often be fed some crushed oats or barley and perhaps a little cake. The system known as barley-beef has made some impact on these farms ; this system will be described later.

The returns from fattening cattle are generally small ; indeed it has been argued that this is one of the surest ways of losing money. Certainly if store cattle are bought and fattened inside, the level of profit will mainly depend on the skill of buying ; the profit in beef, so far as the farmer is concerned, appears to be mainly in rearing. It is impossible to give an average figure for the returns from a beef enterprise : some farmers are showing a profit of around £20 per head, others are making a loss.

SHEEP ON STOCK REARING AND FATTENING FARMS

The major difference in the sheep enterprise on the stock rearing and fattening farms as compared with the stock rearing farms is that the wether lambs are sold fat rather than as stores. The flock will usually be a mountain breed crossed with a longwool, but on the better farms flocks of cross-bred ewes will be found. The source of the cross-bred ewe has already been discussed. These ewes will possess the hardiness of their mountain breed dams and the milkiness, fecundity, and, to a degree, the frame of their longwool sires. In addition to this they will show a degree of *heterosis* or hybrid vigour. Under good conditions, where the ewes can be *flushed* before tupping, a lambing percentage of 180 can be expected. The ewes of a cross-bred flock will be crossed with a down breed for the production of good-quality down cross lambs. At the time of writing the most popular down breed in this context is the Suffolk. This second cross represents the third stage in the system of stratification to which reference has already been made. On this better land 70 per cent of the wether lambs might be expected to be sold fat off the ewe and only 30 per cent should require fattening on roots. The ewe lambs may also be sold fat, but some are sold for crossing, again with a down breed—this time a Hampshire tup is popular. The major disadvantage of the cross-bred flock is that it cannot be self-contained. Thus if the ewes are capable of four crops of lambs, 25 per cent of the flock has to be replaced each year.

There are two main differences between the management of a cross-bred flock and that of a hill flock. Firstly, the ewes are encouraged to give multiple births ; this is achieved by having them in rising condition at the time of mating ; thus they are usually kept on poor pasture after their lambs are weaned in August and then they are brought onto better pasture about two weeks before mating ; this ensures that multiple ova are produced and that a high proportion of twins will be born. Secondly, lambing takes place earlier in the spring ; a cross-bred flock will be expected to start lambing in March and the tups are therefore run with the ewes in October.

Cross-bred ewes are more profitable than the hill flocks and can be expected to give a return of at least £4 per head. The net profit per hectare on these farms shows a wide variation, but on the better farms a figure of £25 would be considered reasonable.

It has already been mentioned that the cropping programme is essentially similar to that on the stock rearing farms. In a typical area in Aberdeen a popular rotation is three years arable and three years ley ; the three years arable comprises oats, roots, oats, though today there is a tendency for barley to be taken as one of the cereal breaks. In this rotation the high proportion of roots is noteworthy.

CHAPTER 4

DAIRY FARMING

WHILST each of the farming systems so far described is concerned dominantly with livestock production and is, in consequence, dependent, at least to some extent, on grassland, the major factors determining the system of farming have consequently been altitude and soil type. Grassland reaches its peak of production at lower altitudes, on strong soil, and in areas of moderate to heavy rainfall. The most profitable utilization of this grass is by the dairy cow. It is not surprising to find that areas of dairy farming have developed in the south west of Scotland, down the west coast of England particularly in the counties of Lancashire and Cheshire, in Staffordshire, Derbyshire, Gloucestershire, Berkshire, Wiltshire, Somerset, Dorset and Central Devon. In other areas the proximity of industry has overridden the dictates of climate and given rise to intensive dairy farming; such areas are found in parts of the north east of England and to the north and south of London. The influence of industry promoting a system of farming in somewhat unfavourable circumstances is well illustrated by the town dairies; today these have been mainly abandoned as a result of the easier transport of liquid milk.

BREEDS OF DAIRY CATTLE

Today the most numerous breed of dairy cattle is the British Friesian; the popularity of this breed lies partly in its high milk yields and partly in its dual-purpose character. Thus the Friesian stirk is capable of being fattened and is particularly well suited to the system of barley-beef. Today the Friesian breed probably produces 60 per cent of the nation's milk and 40 per cent of its home-produced beef; this is despite the fact that it is the youngest of Britain's breeds, having been established some fifty years ago, though cattle from Holland, the source of the breed, were imported in large numbers in the nineteenth century. Next in popularity in the dairy breeds is the Ayrshire which came into existence sometime before the end of the eighteenth century. Whilst the milk yield is not as high as the Friesian the butter fat content is somewhat higher. The breed is particularly well suited to the poorer dairy farms at high elevations and with cold climate. The Dairy Shorthorn, next in numerical importance, is a truly dual-purpose animal: the steers make good beef, and the cow herself will readily fatten at the end of her milking life. The Shorthorn is the oldest of the nation's breeds of cattle and originated in the counties of Durham, Northumberland and Yorkshire. The Channel Island breeds are two in number—the Jersey and the Guernsey. Both are noted for the quality of their milk, and together they are numerically about as important as the Dairy Shorthorn. The South Devon breed, whilst numerically small, is interesting in that it is physically the largest British breed of cattle, and in that its milk qualifies, along with the Jersey and Guernsey, for the " quality premium". Other dairy and dual-purpose breeds are the Kerry, the Dexter, the Lincoln Red Shorthorn, the Red Poll, and the Welsh Black.

Dairying is the backbone of British agriculture and milk production accounts for nearly one-quarter of the total output of farms in this country. Many distinct systems of dairy farming are practised, and these represent various combinations of systems of housing, feeding and herd replacement. Each of these factors of management will be briefly considered.

THE BYRE SYSTEM

Two major systems of housing are practised. The first, most often found on the purely dairy farm, is the traditional byre system where the cows are individually tied up for at least a part of the year. The advocates of this system claim that it gives more opportunity for individual attention, especially as regards feeding, and consequently leads to higher milk yields and a greater margin of value of milk produced over cost of concentrates fed ; it is also sometimes claimed that the byre system gives a greater degree of disease control in that it allows an earlier recognition of the presence of disease. Modern byres incorporate labour-saving devices such as mechanical byre cleaners and pipe line milkers. The mechanical cleaners consist of a conveyor belt running in the manure channel ; two or three times a day the belt is set in motion and it deposits the manure into a waiting manure spreader. With pipeline milking machines, the milk from the teat-cups is carried under vacuum directly to the milk room and can be discharged into a refrigerated bulk tank. This system greatly cuts down the amount of labour involved in handling milk.

THE YARD AND PARLOUR

The other main system of housing is the yard and parlour. Here the cows are loose-housed in bedded yards at least for the major part of the winter. The cows are milked in a parlour adjoining the yard ; parlours vary in size and may hold from 3 to 18 cows. All the equipment is fixed and the cows move through the building during milking. The advocates of this system point out that the labour requirement is low and claim a better health record for cows that are loose-housed. On purely dairy farms the system may be difficult to incorporate because of the high requirement of straw for bedding. A modification of the system is one of cow cubicles representing an intermediate stage between the byre and the yard. In this system the cows are able to go into single standings and to lie down, or to exercise at will. Only the cubicle needs to be bedded, thus effecting a considerable saving in cost, especially in areas where straw is in short supply.

THE BAIL SYSTEM

The bail system of milk production ought to be mentioned whilst considering housing of dairy cows. The milking bail is essentially a milking parlour on wheels. The cows are outside for the whole year and the bail is taken to the field in which they are being kept. This system is most satisfactory in areas with mild winters and on land that does not *poach*; it is particularly useful on large farms where many of the fields being grazed by the dairy herd lie some considerable distance from the steading. A modification to the system is where the dairy herd is housed in yards during the winter and the bail is set up adjacent to the yard, serving the same purpose as the milking parlour. Indeed it is from this system that the yard and parlour developed.

FEEDING DAIRY COWS

Fundamentally the different systems of winter feeding dairy cattle may be divided into one of two groups : (a) low dependence on home-produced foods and a high input of purchased concentrates, or (b) a high dependence on home-produced foods and a low input of purchased concentrates. Home-produced foods are generally bulky and expensive to handle in large quantities ; purchased concentrates on the other hand are easier to feed, cheaper to handle, but more expensive in unit value. Consequently the greater number of byre herds are fed on home-produced foods only for maintenance requirements and perhaps the first or second gallon of milk. With loose-housing, however, the cows can be self-fed on a home-produced food such as silage ; the restriction of their intake is their appetite, rather than the weight of silage that the available labour force can conveniently handle. With self-fed silage of sufficiently high quality the maintenance requirements of the animals will be met together with the requirements for 15–20 litres of milk. Thus purchased concentrate foods will only be fed to cows giving over 20 litres of milk per day; however, with such high-quality silage low-yielding cows are bound to be overfed.

In a similar way the summer feeding of dairy cows may be mainly dependent on grass or the grass may be supplemented by purchased concentrates throughout most of the summer. Thus, with high nitrogenous fertilizer applications, under careful management, and by the strict selection of grass species and the use of various forage crops such as kale, it is possible to provide high-quality grazing not only for the duration of the summer, but even for the greater part of the winter. On the other hand, with less intensive management, the grass will make a significant contribution to milk production for less than three months during the summer.

PROFITABILITY OF DAIRY FARMING

Generally intensive grassland management in the summer is associated with a high dependence on silage and other home-produced feeds in the winter. This is because the utilization of intensive grassland is much simpler if the surplus grass is cut for silage. There is also a tendency for farmers with a yard and parlour system to manage their grassland more intensively than those with a byre system. This combination of yard and parlour and intensive grassland represents a low cost system of milk production, and it would appear that a comparison between the yard and parlour and the byre systems is generally a comparison between low cost–low output and high cost–high output. Typically more cows can be kept on a yard and parlour system, but the profit per cow is lower than on the byre system. Profits for different herds show such a wide variation that it is unwise to be dogmatic about which system leaves the higher profit per hectare. The production of milk can be profitable whether it is produced at a low cost with a low concentrate input and only medium yields, or at high cost with high concentrate input and high yields. Losses are incurred when high inputs are associated with low yields resulting from poor management. The order of profit that can be expected under average management would be £35–£50 per hectare on small farms, and £25–£40 on larger farms; this would represent a profit of about £25 per cow; however, profits of over £50 per cow can be obtained.

HERD REPLACEMENTS

The herd maintenance policy adopted will have little overall effect on the profitability of the enterprise, since newly calved heifers may be purchased at about the same cost as would be incurred if they were reared on the farm. There are three main methods of herd replacement :

(a) Rearing heifer calves.
(b) Buying in newly calved heifers and breeding from them, but selling all the calves. The cows are kept so long as they continue to breed and to milk satisfactorily.
(c) Buying in newly calved heifers or cows and milking them until they fail to give a satisfactory yield. These cows are then sold geld.

Pedigree animals are invariably home reared, as also are many purebred animals. The second system is more commonly found in mixed breed herds, and to a degree in smaller herds of commercial animals. The third system is known as the flying herd system ; this is found less commonly today than it was up to about twenty years ago ; at this time it was the common method of replacement with the town dairies and also, at the other extreme, with the bail milking herds in the south. Today many farmers buy in some of their herd replacements and rear others. Some farmers rear their replacements, not because they feel that it is cheaper to do so, but because they consider that there is less risk of bringing disease onto the farm.

CROPPING ON THE DAIRY FARM

Cropping on a specialized dairy farm will of course be restricted to the production of those crops which are necessary to feed the cows. The rotation adopted will depend on the degree of reliance on home-produced feeds. Thus where maximum use is to be made of forage crops a cow will require about 0·4 hectare for summer grazing, 0·4 hectare for silage and hay, 0·2 hectare of corn and 0·1 hectare of kale, making a total of just over 1 hectare per cow; this amount would be considerably reduced by higher than average fertilizer applications. In this case the rotation would be simply a three- or four-year ley followed by a corn crop which would be undersown with grass seeds to re-establish the ley, the small area of kale forming part of the corn break. Such a farm would be found in the wetter parts of the country, and the corn crops would probably be oats, though today there is a tendency to grow barley even in these districts.

CHAPTER 5

MIXED DAIRYING AND STOCK
REARING FARMS OFTEN
WITH HILL SHEEP

FARMS in this group are in many ways similar either to those described as
dominantly stock rearing or to those described as stock rearing and fattening.
They are typically represented by those dales farms of the Pennines that in
comparatively recent years have developed a dairy enterprise partly because of
economic necessity and partly because of easier access to markets. The majority
of these farms were at one time primarily hill sheep and stock rearing farms, but
today the emphasis is often on dairying. However, with some of the farms,
despite the dairy enterprise, the emphasis is still on sheep.

These farms occur in less favourable areas than the pure dairy farms ; they
have a shorter growing season and the grass is of mediocre quality. If hill
grazings are excluded the areas are usually small. Consequently the dairy
herds are small. These factors result in a system of dairy farming typically
based on byre housing and a high dependence on bought concentrates. Most of
the herd replacements are home reared and often heifers in excess of home
requirements are raised.

The sheep enterprise on such a farm is usually based on the production of
cross-bred lambs. Some of the lower-lying farms may cross ewes of one of the
hill breeds with Down rams ; some may even keep cross-bred ewes and put them
to a Down ram. In any event the sheep enterprise is generally more intensive
than that found on the marginal and hill farms ; thus the lambing percentage is
higher and a higher proportion of the wether lambs are sold fat.

Cropping systems are also similar to the stock rearing and fattening farms,
though there is usually a lesser dependence on leys and a greater dependence on
permanent pastures. The competition between the dairy cattle and the sheep
for the early spring and late autumn grass is a typical feature. The grassland
often shows the ill effects of over-grazing at these times and under-grazing in
the late spring and early summer. Some of the farmers overcome the tendency
by making silage, but it is surprising how many still rely on hay as a method of
grass conservation ; this is despite the fact that, in general, the high rainfall
would suggest that silage would be a more satisfactory method.

47

The composition of the output of such farms mainly depends on whether or not they have common fell grazing rights. Thus, where no common fell grazing rights exist, milk will account for over 50 per cent of the output, cattle for about 20 per cent and sheep for a further 20 per cent; poultry and eggs, particularly the summer trade at the farm door, may account for 5 per cent. If common fell grazing rights do exist the contribution of sheep to the gross output may rise to 30 per cent or even higher, that of cattle may rise to 25 per cent, and that of milk may be less than 40 per cent.

The introduction of the dairy enterprise has generally led to an increase in the profits of the farm; though this is difficult to assess, some indication is given by the figures given in Table 3, quoted from a survey of farming in the North of England (Department of Agricultural Economics, University of Newcastle, Report 153M, 1962).

TABLE 3[1]

Type of farm	Profit per hectare
	£
Upland rearing farms :	
with common fell grazings	2·4
without common fell grazings :	
(a) cross-breeding sheep enterprise	4·3
(b) pure breeding sheep enterprise	1·8
Upland mixed farms :	
with common fell grazing rights	5·0
without common fell grazing rights	18·0

[1] Table originally given in profit per acre.

In interpreting these figures it must be remembered that the profit per hectare fell grazings is, of course, extremely low. A low profit per hectare of farms with fell grazings does not necessarily imply a low farm profit, since the total area involved may be large.

CHAPTER 6

MIXED DAIRYING AND ARABLE FARMS

THESE farms differ from those described under dairy farming in that sale crops
form a significant portion of the gross output. Such farms are not very numerous
in Scotland though they do occur in the east where about 30 per cent of all dairy
farms (about 5 per cent of full time farms in this region) fall into this group.
On the other hand, economic conditions in England and Wales favour this type
of farming and examples are to be found in widespread areas, e.g. South East
Northumberland, the Cumberland coast, around Pontefract in Yorkshire, North
Cheshire, the West Midlands, the fertile valleys of Wales and especially the Vale
of Glamorgan, Shropshire and the Upper Severn Vale, West Warwickshire,
East Worcestershire, parts of the Chilterns, the Vale of Aylesbury, South Essex,
South Hertfordshire, the Weald of Kent, Surrey and Sussex, and areas of
Somerset, Cornwall and Devon.

Size of the farms in this group ranges from 60 hectares to over 600 hectares, the
larger farms tending to occur on the Downlands. The system of dairying also
varies and each of the systems previously described is represented. Thus, in
the midlands and in the north, the byre or the yard and parlour is typical. As a
result of the cash cropping, there is seldom a shortage of straw, and consequently
the recent development of the cow cubicle has not been widely adopted. Until
the last fifty years or so dairying played a very small part on the Downs, and milk
production was practically impossible, partly because the farms were isolated
and partly because of the shortage of water. The traditional method for main-
taining fertility on the rendzina soils was by folding sheep. But during the
Second World War the labour required for looking after arable sheep flocks was
not available ; even before this the Milk Marketing Board had started to collect
milk daily from any farm, however remote, and grants were made available for
farm water supplies. All these factors led to the system of bail milking and open
air dairying, and today the cow has often replaced the sheep in its rôle of main-
taining fertility and enabling satisfactory yields of grain to be maintained.

ALTERNATE HUSBANDRY

Though the details of keeping dairy cows may vary from district to district
within the group of farms, the application of the principles of alternate husbandry
remains common to nearly all of them. Thus with few exceptions grassland
husbandry is dominated by the ley, i.e. land that is put down to grass for a

specified period up to seven or ten years; there is generally less permanent pasture on these farms than on any other system so far considered. The benefits of alternate husbandry may be summarized as follows:

(a) It has often been pointed out that soil structure is the key to soil fertility; of all the cultivations that a farmer carries out, ploughing is the only one that can be said to improve soil structure. Under long periods of cropping, therefore, the structure of the soil is gradually weakened and this leads to a decrease in fertility and lower crop yields; in the extreme case this can lead to soil erosion on a disastrous scale, e.g. the Kansas Dust Bowl. The structure of the soil is built up in a number of ways, but one of the most effective is by grass roots: evidence of this is to be seen in the strongly structured A horizons of the Chernozems. One of the main objects of alternate husbandry is to allow the structure of the soil to be built up under a period of grass so that it can withstand cash-cropping for a number of years.

(b) Associated with this decline in soil structure during a period of cropping is the equally important fall in the organic matter content of the soil. Organic matter is important to the soil for a number of reasons:

    (i) It releases nitrogen and other plant foods; the *fixation* of phosphate may well be less of a problem in soils with a high organic matter content.

    (ii) It is about five times as effective, weight for weight, as clay, so far as cation exchange reactions are concerned. Cation exchange is the physico-chemical reaction whereby plant nutrients are held in the soil and subsequently released for the plant; the major cations concerned are calcium, magnesium, potassium and sodium.

    (iii) It imparts to the soil a dark colour; and since dark surfaces absorb more heat and reflect less than light surfaces, a soil with a high organic content warms up quicker in the spring and is consequently earlier in promoting growth.

    (iv) It is capable of holding moisture. Soils with high organic contents are therefore less susceptible to drought; at the same time, owing to the promotion of soil structure, they are more readily drained.

It is evident that organic matter is of equal importance to heavy soils and to light soils. Thus it opens up heavy soils, making them easier to cultivate, better drained and warmer; it binds together the coarser particles of light sandy soils, making them less liable to erosion or to drought.

(c) The control of many plant diseases is more readily achieved under a system of alternate husbandry. Examples of such diseases are Take-all or Whiteheads in cereals, and a number of root eelworm diseases. This is because the inclusion of a ley in the rotation lengthens the rotation and thus gives a better separation in time between crops of related species.

(d) If the ley contains clover the nitrogen content of the soil is built up by the action of symbiosis : certain bacteria, capable of manufacturing organic compounds from the nitrogen of the air, live on the roots of clover and other legumes ; nitrates are released to the subsequent crop when the ley is ploughed. This means that less nitrogenous fertilizer need be applied to a crop following a ley than one following, for example, a cereal crop. The real contribution of the ley to the nutrition of the following crop depends on many factors, the more important of which are the percentage clover in the ley and the management of the ley. It has been estimated that the quality of nitrogen fixed under average conditions is equivalent to about 600 kg of sulphate of ammonia per hectare, but all of this may not in fact be available in the year following ploughing. In practice the nitrogen application to a cereal crop following a ley should not be reduced by more than the equivalent of 250 kg of sulphate of ammonia.

(e) In general terms the productivity of a ley is greater than that of a permanent pasture. It may therefore be supposed that alternate husbandry or ley farming leads to an intensification of the livestock enterprises. That this is generally true is beyond dispute, but the major reason may well lie not in the ley *per se*, but rather in the normally low standard of management to which the majority of permanent pastures are subjected. It is true that leys consisting of one or two species of grass are easier to manage than permanent pastures consisting of many species ; but the generally lower productivity of permanent grassland results from the failure of the average farmer to adopt a system of grassland management that will maintain the more valuable species and allow them to give of their best.

Alternate husbandry is not without its disadvantages. On large farms the distance from the steading to the more distant fields may make them unsuitable for grazing ; this can unduly complicate grassland management, where the climate is unsuitable for open air dairying and bail milking. Again, if the ley is to be established under a cereal crop (undersown), complications may be experienced when the cereal is harvested. If the ley is established by direct seeding low productivity in the first year may result.

ROTATIONS ON MIXED DAIRY AND ARABLE FARMS

On some mixed dairy and arable farms two rotations are adopted : one for the fields nearest the building where the ley is the pivot of the rotation, and a second for the fields farther from the building where the emphasis is on cereal growing. The first rotation will be similar to that described for pure dairy farms, and the second will be similar to that to be described shortly for dominantly arable farms. The system may well lead to a simplification of management, but most of the advantages of alternate husbandry are lost.

The rotation adopted under alternate husbandry will often be a modification of the classical Norfolk four-course :

> 1st year : Wheat
>
> 2nd year : Roots
>
> 3rd year : Barley
>
> 4th year : Seeds

Today the ley is most often extended to three or four years, thus reducing the quantity of roots. Sometimes two white crops (cereals) will be taken after the ley, a practice that is increasing under the present economic régime of high profits from cereals. In the original four-course rotation the root crop was generally turnips, but today turnips are often considered an expensive luxury and potatoes or sugar beet are more usually grown. Despite these modifications many of the advantages of the Norfolk four-course rotation remain and these may be briefly summarized :

(a) The principles of alternate husbandry with the resulting benefits previously described are obtained.

(b) The demand for labour is more or less evenly spread throughout the year.

(c) The advantages of a diversity of enterprise are realized. Thus a year that is bad for cereal growing will most often be good for potatoes, sugar beet, and grassland. On the other hand, if a dry season is experienced and the output from grass and most crops is low, the increased cereal yields will often compensate.

PROFITABILITY

The profitability of a mixed dairy and arable farm will depend to a large extent on the distribution of the gross output between milk and cash crops. Surveys have repeatedly shown that in the present economic climate the profit per hectare is greater with arable farming than with livestock. Thus under good management a profit of £55 per hectare could be expected on an arable farm, whereas £46 per hectare would be considered good on a dairy farm. On really fertile soil with potatoes and sugar beet as a part of the rotation and with intensively managed grassland, profits of £35–£50 per hectare can be averaged; on lighter land of lower fertility where a greater reliance must be placed on the ley, profits of £20–£25 per hectare may be a more reasonable standard.

CHAPTER 7

MIXED DAIRYING AND FATTENING
FARMS WITH SOME
ARABLE LAND

WITH alternate husbandry systems the ley may be utilized in ways other than for dairy farming. In many cases sheep are an additional enterprise and on some farms fattening cattle are also carried. Fat cattle and dairy farms are found in the well-known grazing areas of Northamptonshire and Leicestershire, and also in South Northumberland and along the Northumberland coast. In South Durham and North Yorkshire and in some areas of Oxfordshire and North-amptonshire there are farms where fat cattle, sheep, milk and cash cropping are all included and it is difficult to name any one enterprise as being dominant. On the larger farms of the chalk lands of South Central England (parts of Wiltshire, Hampshire, Berkshire and Dorset and including the South Downs and, to a less extent, the North Downs and the Cotswolds), corn production is the dominant enterprise with both sheep and dairying utilizing the leys.

The farms in this group bear a close affinity, both geographically and agriculturally, to those in the previous group. Thus they occur in similar regions, and in both cases the system is based on alternate husbandry. The dairy enterprises and the arable cropping show similar patterns to those described above, and the main distinction is the addition of either a beef enterprise or a sheep enterprise, or both.

WINTER FEEDING OF BEEF CATTLE
In the past, winter feeding of beef cattle in yards or byres resulted in the production of much first class beef. However, today many of the yards designed for beef cattle have been adapted for milk production by the addition of milking parlours. It is mainly on farms where the buildings cannot be readily brought up to the standards required by the Milk and Dairies Order that beef production continues ; notwithstanding this general statement, there are still some arable farms where winter fed beef are kept almost entirely as a means of converting surplus straw into farmyard manure.

Cattle intended for winter fattening are generally well-grown and mature Irish stores, of the type already discussed. The classical English or Norfolk

53

system of feeding cattle was a natural outcome of the Norfolk four-course rotation where 25 per cent of the land was devoted to turnips. Cattle were fed large quantities of turnips, up to 100 kg/day, a little hay, and 2 or 2·5 kg of concentrates. Such a system maintained the fertility of the soil by the supply of farmyard manure, kept the land clean through the inter-row cultivations to which the turnip crop was subjected, and made a significant contribution to the beef supply of the nation. However, today artificial fertilizers can, at least to some extent, replace farmyard manure, and selective weed killers are an efficient aid in keeping the land clean. Labour is an expensive item, and turnips have a high labour demand. It is for these reasons that the practice of feeding cattle by the Norfolk system is no longer widespread. Much research has therefore been directed towards developing a system of fattening cattle by a less expensive and a less laborious method.

Thus in recent years the possibilities of silage as a replacement for turnips have been considered, and comparative trials have been conducted at two main centres—Aberdeen and Belfast. In all these trials silage has been shown to be a real alternative to roots, giving a satisfactory live weight gain and a good quality carcass at slaughter. A number of farmers in the above-defined areas have now adopted this practice.

BARLEY BEEF

An even more recent development is that of beef from barley. This system has been studied in this country mainly at the Rowett Research Institute, Aberdeen. Essentially the system is similar to the beef batteries of the United States ; the animals are fattened entirely on concentrates, and without the use of roughages ; the concentrates consist of about 85 per cent of barley and are given *ad libitum*; the cattle are housed in yards and the aim is to have them fattened in less than twelve months. Such an intensive system may well have possibilities in the traditional sheep and barley areas, and certainly the financial statements are promising : profits of around £20 per head have been reported. The system would appear to be particularly suited to the mixed farms here discussed since cross-bred stock from the dairy breeds, and especially the Friesian, have been shown to respond particularly well. Indeed much of the work so far reported has been carried out either with pure bred Friesian stirks or with Friesian cross Hereford stock.

Whilst the traditional methods of winter fattening can rightly be regarded as in the main unprofitable, summer fed beef is much cheaper to produce and it is generally agreed that beef can be obtained from grass at a profit. However, summer fattening is of less importance in the context of the system of farming here discussed, since compared to dairying or sheep it is a much less efficient method of utilizing leys. Where dairying and beef co-exist as enterprises on a particular farm, the beef enterprise is most often one of beef from the dairy herd, and only occasionally are these animals summer fattened. Summer fattening will therefore be considered under mixed fattening and arable farms.

SHEEP ON THE MIXED DAIRYING, FATTENING AND ARABLE FARMS

On mixed dairying, fattening and arable farms the sheep enterprise usually comprises the production of fat lambs from cross-bred ewes. The management of these flocks is generally similar to that for the cross-bred flocks described for stock rearing and fattening farms. There are, however, three possible differences, resulting in part from the greater intensity of the enterprise. Thus the flock may represent a fourth stage in stratification, and second cross (often Suffolk cross Half-bred) ewe lambs may be bought in and crossed with a Hampshire ram ; in this case a lambing percentage of at least 180 would be expected and 90 per cent of the lambs should go fat off the ewe, with 10 per cent or even less being root fed.

The second difference is that the lambs are often creep grazed. This means that the field is divided into six or eight paddocks and the sheep flock is rotated round these paddocks. The lambs always have access to the paddock ahead of the ewes, but at the same time they are able to run back with their mothers. This is an intensive form of sheep production, and up to 25 ewes and their lambs can be carried per hectare throughout the summer. With such a system profits of £40 per hectare can be achieved.

The third difference is that the flock may be one of the grassland breeds instead of a cross-bred flock. The most popular of the grassland ewes at the present time is probably the Clun Forest, though the Kerry Hill comes a close second. The essential difference in management between a flock of a grassland breed and a cross-bred flock is that whereas in the former only rams need to be bought in, in the latter a number of ewes must also be replaced each year.

PROFITABILITY

The profits from a system of farming based on dairying, fattening, and arable enterprises can be expected to be of the same order as those from the dairying and arable farms ; they will again depend mainly on the distribution of the output between the enterprises and especially between arable and grassland products. Since traditional winter fattening will make little direct contribution to the overall profit the greater the emphasis that is placed on this enterprise the lower will be the profit per hectare; on the other hand, the most profitable method of disposing of barley may be through intensive beef production ; and the practice of such a system will generally lead to an increase in overall profit from the farm.

E

CHAPTER 8

MIXED FATTENING AND ARABLE FARMS

WITHIN this group are included many farms in the traditional sheep and barley areas where conditions are unfavourable for the introduction of dairying. Such areas are found in parts of the Yorkshire and Lincolnshire Wolds, the magnesian limestone of North East Derbyshire, the South Lincolnshire limestone areas, and the sandy areas of Nottinghamshire. Also included are the sheep and barley farms where other cash crops are grown—such as are found in some areas of the East Riding, parts of North Lincolnshire, South Cambridgeshire, North and West Norfolk and East Suffolk. In other parts of Lincolnshire, West Huntingdonshire and Bedfordshire, in Leicestershire, North East Northumberland and around North Berwick where the soil is dominantly clay, the main enterprises are fat cattle and wheat. In the Merse of Berwick, and in Angus, along the southern shore of the Firth of Forth, in the Carses of Gowrie and Stirling and scattered over the greater part of Aberdeenshire, a system of farming based on fat cattle, sheep and cereals is followed. Farms following this system occupy the best arable land in Scotland. On the other hand, it can be seen that mixed fattening and arable farms are also to be found either on light land or on clay land. In both cases they owe their development to the ameliorating effect of the ley and of farmyard manure on soils that would otherwise be unsuitable for a wide range of crops.

SUMMER FATTENING OF BEEF CATTLE

Many of these farmers practise both winter and summer fattening. The system of winter fattening is essentially the same as that described for the mixed dairying, fattening, and arable farms. The more profitable system of beef production is summer fattening, and cattle intended for this system are best kept on a low plane of nutrition in the previous winter. On some farms store cattle are bought in at about eighteen months of age in the autumn, kept during the winter in store condition on hay, straw and a few roots or a little silage, and turned out to grass in the spring. In other cases the majority of the cattle required for grazing will be bought in the spring when they are about two years of age. The choice will depend partly on the supply and market price of stores in the autumn and in the spring, and partly on the building available for wintering. Store cattle are more expensive in the spring, but the difference in

56

value may not be sufficient to cover the cost of wintering. Many farmers winter sufficient cattle to utilize the spring grass and then buy in additional stores in the early summer, so that the density of stocking keeps pace with the rate of growth of the grass. As the rate of growth of the grass declines, so are the cattle sold fat. This adjustment of stocking has maintained the productivity of the fattening pastures of Leicestershire and North East Northumberland.

Notwithstanding the previous discussion of the value of alternate husbandry to arable crops, the best summer fattening pastures are almost certainly permanent grass. But the area covered by permanent grass of sufficiently high quality to fatten even 2 beasts to the hectare is very small, and over recent years much more attention has been paid to the use of temporary grass for this purpose. This is especially so in Scotland, where for over a century the value of the ley has been recognized. Where dairying is impracticable, but alternate husbandry is desirable, the utilization of the ley by summer fattening may have its attractions. However, the profit from such a system, even where two and a half beasts are fattened on every hectare, will seldom exceed £15 per hectare; this compares very unfavourably with other outlets for the ley or, for that matter, with other more intensive methods of producing beef.

SHEEP AND BARLEY FARMS

It has already been indicated that on much of the traditional sheep and barley land sheep have been replaced by dairy cows. However, there are still some farms that maintain an arable sheep flock, and these farms are included in the group here discussed. In this system the flock is confined by wooden or wicker hurdles on a limited area of fodder crops. When this small area is eaten off the flock moves on to a fresh fold. In its most intensive form, lamb creeps are provided to allow the lambs to creep ahead of the ewes, much as is done in forward creep grazing ; the flock is moved daily, and special rotations may be adopted to provide a continuous succession of crops for folding.

Where the system is practised today, folding is most often employed only in the late autumn and winter when the sheep are run on beet tops, kale or rape ; during the summer, they are grazed on leys. Traditionally the down breeds have been the main breeds for arable sheep flocks, and many of the down flocks kept for breeding rams are still managed on this system. Of local interest is the longwool breed, the English Leicester, which is found in arable flocks in the East Riding. The traditional system of arable sheep farming has some advantages : it permits a high rate of stocking since the frequency of ploughing prevents a build up of parasitic worms in the soil. Abundance of winter food permits early lambing, even in late December, and thus lends itself to the production of early fat lambs. It is an intensive system with a high output per hectare and it gives appreciable indirect returns in the increased yields of corn on land that has held a folded flock. But the advantages of the system, except in the case of specialized ram producing flocks, are outweighed by the major disadvantage of a high labour demand, and there is little doubt but that the system is now outdated and unprofitable.

Today ewe flocks are usually maintained on permanent grass or on leys associated with arable farming, but with provision for winter feeding on kale or roots where appropriate. The management and profitability of these flocks are generally similar to those described for sheep under mixed dairying, fattening, and arable farms.

CROPPING ON MIXED FATTENING AND ARABLE FARMS

The rotation adopted for mixed fattening and arable farms will depend on the district, and on the necessity for providing winter feed. An example of a rotation where an arable sheep flock was carried would be wheat, winter corn and vetches, swedes, rape and turnips, wheat, oats, two years ryegrass and clover ; such a rotation would seldom be found today. A more common rotation on the Downs would be wheat, barley, barley, three years ley; a small quantity of roots may be included. In moister areas both potatoes and sugar beet may be grown and the rotation could be potatoes, wheat, sugar beet, barley, three years ley. The traditional East Lothian rotation is roots, barley, seeds, oats, potatoes, wheat.

The profitability of this system of farming will largely depend on the relative importance of livestock and of cash crops. Generally the profit per hectare will be lower than that of the mixed dairying and arable farms, because the profitability of livestock fattening is less than that of dairying. On many farms profits of £15–£20 are considered reasonable and this figure would apply to chalk land farms or to mixed fattening and arable farms on stronger land. On the more intensive farms profits of £50 per hectare or more can be obtained.

CHAPTER 9

DOMINANTLY ARABLE FARMS

A SMALL number of dominantly arable farms are found in the east and south west of Scotland, but the more important areas of Great Britain where this system is found are in the Fens of Lincolnshire, Cambridgeshire, Norfolk, and the Isle of Ely. Other fen areas are found in the Plain of Lancastria. Many of the farms in Norfolk and Suffolk are predominantly arable, and East Anglia has often been referred to as the grain farm of Great Britain ; other areas are the Suffolk–Essex area of boulder clay, South Yorkshire and the Holderness area.

For the most part the land under this system of farming is the most fertile in the country, though some less fertile heavy land is also included. The system varies in this group from region to region, depending in part on the local soil conditions and in part on the local climate ; such variations take the form of differences in emphasis on various crops and in the relative importance of livestock enterprises, though by definition, livestock on these farms is always subsidiary to the production of cash crops.

CROPS AND SOIL TYPE

The suitability of a crop to a particular soil type is not a clear cut issue. There are many varieties of most crops, and in many cases different varieties show preferences for different types of soil. However, a broad classification can be made : thus wheat, potatoes, sugar beet and market garden crops are particularly suited to Fens and Silts ; barley, sugar beet, market garden crops and short leys are suited to light soils and to chalk soils ; lucerne is also particularly suited to chalk soils and good yields of potatoes can be had from light soils ; wheat, oats, beans and longer leys are preferred for heavy soils, whereas practically all crops can yield well on loams. For any crop the lighter the rainfall, the heavier is the soil on which it will do best ; the converse is also true. But, as has been indicated earlier, factors other than soil and climate must be considered in deciding whether a crop is suited to a particular farm ; thus the proximity of a sugar beet factory would encourage large areas of this crop in the rotation possibly at the expense of potatoes—a crop for which the land may be more suited. The large acreage of potatoes on heavy land in Essex, grown because of the proximity of the market in London, is another example of geographical location overriding the dictates of soil and climatic conditions.

Within this type of farming there are therefore a number of different rotations adopted, though it ought to be noted that in recent years the design of cropping systems has contained a considerable element of opportunism, and rigid crop rotations are by no means common. This was not always so : prior to 1874 the lease of a tenant farmer would usually prescribe the rotation which he must follow. Similar reservations to those made in classifying crops for different textured soils apply to statements on rotations in particular areas.

THE FENLANDS AND EAST ANGLIA

The Fens of Lincolnshire, Cambridgeshire, the Isle of Ely and West Norfolk probably contribute the largest area of land of uniform high fertility in this country. Two types of soil are here included—the true fens or the Black Fen covering about 142,000 hectares, and about the same area of silts. The true fens have been reclaimed from boggy land, lying below the high tide of sea level. This was accomplished by the construction of sea walls and building up of river banks, together with extensive dykes feeding main water courses by pumps. The fields in Fen country are long and narrow to facilitate the construction of drainage ditches, which mainly form the field boundaries. There are no hedges and almost no cattle. Fen land consists largely of mild peat and is highly fertile and dark in colour ; it yields well but quality is not always high. Almost a third of the area is devoted to potato growing, and yields approaching 50 tonnes to the hectare can be obtained: indeed the average yield is probably double that of the remainder of the country. A typical rotation is wheat, potatoes, sugar beet ; but fen soils are also very suited to the growth of vegetable crops such as cauliflowers, cabbages, broccoli, carrots and onions. Today there is a tendency to have a more equal division between roots and cereals.

The silts lie between the true fens and the sea ; they are as fertile as the Black Fen and they are generally deeper ; they are lighter in colour and more easily drained. In consequence there are fewer pumping stations and a less complicated dyke system on silt soils ; such pumping stations as there are occur only on the lowest lying land. The proportion of clay with the silt varies considerably, and some of the silty soils are rather heavy. The higher the proportion of clay, the better do the soils withstand drought ; the lighter soils, however, are generally easier to cultivate, especially after rain. Despite the depth of the silt it is seldom ploughed at more than 38 cm; the silt was deposited from the sea and as deposited is potentially, rather than naturally, fertile, requiring the addition of organic matter before it will support intensive cropping. If the land is deep ploughed raw silt is brought to the surface and this may require two years or even longer before it will grow a good crop.

The silt soils will grow almost any crop well ; yields are as high or higher than on the Black Fen, and the quality is higher. Farmers naturally concentrate on high value cash crops including fruit and bulbs. Peas, carrots, brown mustard and linseed are all grown, but the typical rotation is again wheat, potatoes and sugar beet ; indeed about one-sixth of the national potato crop is grown in this area. Garden varieties of peas are grown on a field scale, often under contract to one of the processing firms. Wheat yields are consistently high and there is less danger of " lodging " than there is on the Black Fen.

There are other areas of fen peat in Great Britain. Of these, the most important is in the Ormskirk region of Lancashire. Here the peat is more acid than it is in the Black Fen around the Wash, and lime has to be applied more frequently—a result of the higher rainfall. Cropping is essentially similar, and again there is an emphasis on potatoes. A further similarity between the three areas—the Black Fen, the silts, and the Plain of Lancastria—is the scarcity of livestock.

In East Norfolk and Suffolk the soil is of a very different nature. Many of the farms are of the type earlier described as mixed fattening and arable, but some are dominantly arable with little livestock. Here the emphasis is on corn rather than on potatoes, and a typical rotation would entail at least half and often two-thirds of the land under corn. An example of a six-course rotation would be wheat, barley, roots, barley, barley, clover ; in some cases a four-course rotation of wheat, roots, barley, clover is favoured. The roots may be potatoes, but are more often sugar beet. In recent years barley has gained in popularity and some farms follow a system of continuous barley growing, though this is more popular on the chalk land of the Downs and of the Wolds.

HEAVY LAND ARABLE FARMING

In the Holderness area of Yorkshire and the clay lands of the borders of Suffolk and Essex, in West Cambridgeshire and East Huntingdonshire heavy land arable farming is found. In certain respects these areas bear a relationship to some of the mixed fattening and arable farms earlier described. But the farms included in this type have a much greater proportion of their land under arable cropping. Often the presence of organic remains from the forests that once covered the land ameliorate the clay, and allow a greater emphasis on arable farming. In these areas the emphasis is usually on wheat and it is not uncommon for a third or even half of the total area to be devoted to this crop; a possible rotation would be wheat, wheat, beans, wheat, oats, clover.

EAST LOTHIAN

In East Lothian, on some of the Old Red Sandstone soils, a system of farming reminiscent of the Fens can be found. These soils have long been famed for their suitability for potato growing, and a rotation is followed in which one-third of the area is devoted to this crop or other root crops. Such a rotation would be oats, potatoes, wheat, roots, barley, seeds. Similar areas are found on the alluvial soils of Perth, Fife, and Angus. Cropping with little or no livestock farms are also found in the south west of Scotland, but these mainly owe their origin to the proximity of Glasgow and the former presence in that city of town byres ; thus the sale of oats, hay, straw, and turnips to these town byres and to stables was a major source of the farm income.

PROFITABILITY OF ARABLE FARMING

The profitability of arable farming is generally high. Thus on large arable farms in East and South East Scotland where sale crops account for 80 per cent of the total farm output, a profit of £50 per hectare can be expected. In the Eastern Counties on the poorer and lighter soils the figure would probably be about £30 per hectare, but on the richer fen soils and silts profits of £125–£150 can be obtained.

CHAPTER 10

HORTICULTURE AND MARKET GARDENING

ALMOST 5 per cent of the total area under crops and rotational grass in Great Britain is devoted to horticulture or market gardening, and this area contributes about 10 per cent to the total agricultural output. The area devoted to horticulture is approximately one-third of that devoted to wheat, but the output is greater than the total output from grain ; in fact the output is over 50 per cent of that from all farm crops.

Important areas for horticulture occur in Scotland. Thus the suitability of soil and climate makes raspberries especially important in Strathmore, where almost 75 per cent of the total production of this fruit in Great Britain is located. On the other hand, there is only a small quantity of top fruit, and this is found mainly around Perth and between Lanark and Glasgow. Market gardens are concentrated around the major cities and in the Lothians. The production of tomatoes is of importance north and east of Lanark and to some extent around Ayr ; in these areas it is the most important crop on the horticulture holdings.

In England the main horticultural and market gardening areas are in the Lea Valley north of London, the Vale of Evesham south of Birmingham, the Biggleswade–Potton area of Bedfordshire, the Wisbech and the Cottenham area of Cambridgeshire, the Botley area in Hampshire, Dartford and Swanley in Kent, Ormskirk in Lancashire, the Tamar Valley on the borders of Devon and Cornwall, and the area from Truro to Penzance.

The main areas for fruit growing are the Vale of Evesham in Worcestershire and Swanley in Kent. The Lea Valley has a concentration of glass, with about 250 hectares—well over 10 per cent of the total area found in England and Wales. The Cottingham district of the East Riding is famed for Dutch light market gardening, and the Leeds district for its rhubarb. Hop growing is confined to two areas, the more famous being on Kent–Sussex borders and the other on the Hereford–Worcester borders. Extensive market gardening and particularly the production of winter cauliflowers are associated with Cornwall. The specialized cultivation of mushrooms is found in the Yaxley district of the Soke of Peterborough.

Horticulture is generally confined to the lighter soils ; it is not essential that they should be naturally fertile since the horticulturist is prepared to make up any deficiency in liberal applications of fertilizers and manures. At one time the industry was largely dependent on the manure from town stables and byres that could be brought back to the land from the markets ; in fact it was once thought that the end of the stables and byres would be the end of intensive market gardening. In the event, fertility has been adequately maintained by the use of artificial fertilizers and organic manures such as *shoddy* and home-made composts ; in some cases green crops of mustard or lupins are grown for ploughing in, thus helping to maintain the organic status of the soil. In still other cases pigs are carried, which serve the dual purpose of utilizing unmarketable material and of providing farmyard manure. These measures, together with the use of transport, have meant that horticulture is no longer restricted to the environs of towns and many large enterprises are found far into the remoter country.

The common difference between all aspects of horticulture and of agriculture is a difference of intensity. Thus the investment per hectare is extremely high depending of course on the utilization of the land. A hectare of glass may demand an investment of up to £60,000 (£25,000 per acre)—about 100 times that required for a mixed farm. Even where the main enterprise is vegetable and soft fruit production, the investment will be much higher than on a typical arable farm; this is partly because of the higher initial cost of horticultural land, partly because of the higher outlay on equipment and machines, partly because of higher applications of fertilizer, and partly because of a greater labour requirement. The output from horticulture is correspondingly higher than that from agriculture; but the horticulturist has no marketing board to protect him, and the risks are so much the greater.

CHAPTER 11

PIGS AND POULTRY

PIGS and poultry are essentially different from other agricultural enterprises since they normally occupy only a small area of land. Both often form subsidiary enterprises on farms mainly devoted to other systems of production, and both lend themselves to a high degree of intensification.

Specialized poultry farms are few in number in Scotland, being found mainly in the south west, especially in North Ayrshire and mid-Lanarkshire. The development of the poultry industry from the days of the barnyard fowl to present-day systems of intensive production has to some extent been centred in Lancashire ; this is partly because of the proximity of the industrial area and partly because of the presence of ports where imported feeding stuffs are landed. Many specialized poultry farms are also found in the Home Counties and in East Anglia. Yet the poultry kept on farms specializing in other branches of agriculture still make a major contribution to the national output of eggs and table birds. The highest density of poultry is found on the dairy farms, and to a less extent on the horticulture and market gardening units. This fact is related to the one-time widespread practice of dairy farms in industrial regions supplying both eggs and milk through retail rounds.

SYSTEMS OF POULTRY MANAGEMENT

Four distinct systems of flock management are practised :

(a) Free range where the birds are allowed to roam over pasture, stubble, and around the environs of the farm ; these birds are usually housed at night.

(b) Fold units ; consisting of small houses or arks to which wire runs are attached ; these units are moved at regular intervals.

(c) Battery houses which are well suited to the specialist producer, and are often found on mixed farms where a specialist poultry unit is maintained. Modern batteries consist of tiers of cages in which one or two birds are kept. Automatic feeding, watering, and cleaning out are often included. Such a system allows a high concentration of birds in a given area and is associated with high levels of egg production. Feed costs and labour costs are higher than on free range, but the higher production gives a greater profit per bird.

(d) Deep litter where the birds are kept in special laying houses on a litter of sawdust or peat moss. About 0·3 square metre is allowed per bird and they are fed *ad libitum*. This is a semi-intensive method and compromises between the high production of the battery and the low capital demand of folded flocks.

The profit per dozen eggs is about the same for battery and deep litter ; free range is much less profitable than any other system. The profit per bird is generally a little higher on the battery systems than on deep litter and may be almost double that for free range; 75–85p per bird per annum would be a reasonable profit on a battery system.

PIG FARMING

As with poultry, pigs may be kept either as a specialized enterprise on a pig farm or as a subsidiary enterprise on a farm specializing in other forms of production. Again pig keeping is in general a dispersed enterprise, but there is a tendency to concentration in East Anglia and also in Middlesex. Very few specialized pig farms are found in Scotland. The highest pig density of any type of farming is found in the market gardens for the reasons given above (p. 64). On most farms pigs can be fitted into the system with reasonable ease. In some cases buildings have been relatively cheaply adapted, and in others special houses, sometimes with *controlled environment*, have been built; often the pig enterprise is a way of utilizing labour that would not otherwise be fully employed.

However, competition in both pigs and poultry is strong, not only from other producers in this country, but also from overseas where producers have evolved very efficient production methods. A high level of efficiency is essential to meet this competition, and the days of reasonable profits from farmyard flocks and pigs kept in basically unsuitable buildings belong to the past. Yet increases in the size of pig and poultry units may well be the only means available to many small farmers of increasing their incomes to a level commensurate with a reasonable standard of living.

BIBLIOGRAPHY

AGRICULTURAL RESEARCH COUNCIL. *Reports of the Soil Survey of Great Britain.* H.M.S.O.
ATTWOOD, E. A. and EVANS, H. G. *The Economics of Hill Farming.* Cardiff (1961).
CENTRAL OFFICE OF INFORMATION. *Agriculture in Britain.* H.M.S.O. (1961).
DEPARTMENT OF AGRICULTURE FOR SCOTLAND. *Types of Farming in Scotland.* H.M.S.O. (1952).
DUDLEY STAMP, L. and BEAVER, S. H. *The British Isles.* Longmans (1964).
FALLEY, R. R. *Commercial Horticulture in Britain.* Wye (1960).
FREAM, W. (ed.). *Elements of Agriculture.* R.A.S.E. (1962).
HIRSCH, G. P. and HUNT, K. E. *British Agriculture.* N.F.Y.F.C. (1957).
KAY GRESSWELL, R. *The Weather and Climate of the British Isles.* Hulton (1961).
McCONNELL, P. *The Agricultural Notebook,* edited by H. I. Moore. Farmer and Stock-Breeder (1958).
MINISTRY OF AGRICULTURE, FISHERIES AND FOOD. *Agriculture: The Journal of the Ministry of Agriculture.* H.M.S.O.
MINISTRY OF AGRICULTURE, FISHERIES AND FOOD. *National Farm Survey of England and Wales.* H.M.S.O. (1946).
RASTALL, R. H. *Agricultural Geology.* Cambridge University Press (1922).
WATSON, Sir J. A. and MORE, J. A. *Agriculture; Science and Practice of British Agriculture.* Oliver and Boyd (1962).

The Agriculture of Scotland and the Border Country

INTRODUCTION

AN IMPORTANT characteristic of the vast majority of the farming systems of Scotland is their dependence on livestock production. This is illustrated by the fact that in 1957, of the total area of agricultural land in Scotland only 20·4 per

FIG. 7. Farming regions in Scotland.

cent was devoted to arable crops ; this compares with 49·8 per cent in England and 37·0 per cent in the whole of Great Britain. On the other hand, much of Scotland is rough grazing of low agricultural value—71·4 per cent of its total agricultural land as compared with 13·4 per cent in England and 35·7 per cent

F

in Great Britain. As a result, despite the fact that almost a third of Great Britain's agricultural land is in Scotland, it carries only 18 per cent of the nation's cattle and 33 per cent of its sheep. The production of fodder crops is closely related to this dependence on livestock, and the main crops are rotation grass, oats, potatoes, turnips, and swedes : nevertheless, there are a number of large farms where arable cropping is the predominant enterprise.

As far as farming systems are concerned six regions can be recognized in Scotland (see Fig. 7) :

(1) The north east stock rearing and feeding areas of Aberdeen, Caithness and the Orkneys.

(2) The eastern coastal strip as far north as Aberdeen, and the Laich of Moray.

(3) The Central Lowlands south of the Highland Boundary Fault and north of the Southern Upland Fault.

(4) South West Scotland including Wigtownshire, Kirkcudbright, Dumfriesshire and Southern Ayrshire.

(5) The North West and Central Highlands.

(6) The Border Country.

CHAPTER 1

THE NORTH EAST STOCK REARING, AND THE STOCK REARING AND FATTENING AREAS

STOCK rearing farms and stock rearing and fattening farms account for about 70 per cent of the full-time farms in the north east of Scotland ; about 60 per cent of all the farms of these types in Scotland are found in this region. In general, stock rearing and feeding farms are found on the lower ground in eastern Aberdeen, whereas stock rearing is the dominant enterprise in the upland areas of Aberdeen, Moray, and Nairn, in the Black Isle of Ross and Cromarty, and in the Orkney Islands. As would be expected, dairy farming has developed in the vicinities of Aberdeen, Peterhead, Fraserburgh, Wick, Thurso, and also around Kirkwall on the mainland of the Orkney Islands.

GEOLOGY AND SOILS

The majority of the region is underlain with Dalradian metamorphic rocks or with granite, though there is an area of Old Red Sandstone running north and south to the east of Turriff. The Orkney Islands and the area around Wick is dominantly Old Red Sandstone. Where the soils are sedentary (i.e. formed *in situ* directly from the underlying rock) they reflect the nature of the solid geology : the soils formed from granite are usually thin, acid, coarse sandy loams ; those formed from Old Red Sandstone are generally red or red-brown, sandy loams to loams. The majority of the region is covered by glacial till, by fluvioglacial sands and gravels, or by mounds of morainic sands and gravels. The soils derived from these deposits again reflect the nature of the parent material : where the till is derived from granite or granitic gneiss the associated soil is generally a gritty sandy loam or a sandy clay loam ; the soils tend to be more loamy in texture if there is a proportion of Old Red Sandstone material in the till ; soils developed on fluvioglacial sands are very sandy and typically of low fertility. Of the Great Soil Groups, Podzols, Brown Forest soils, Non-calcareous gleys, and Peaty gleys are all represented in these areas.

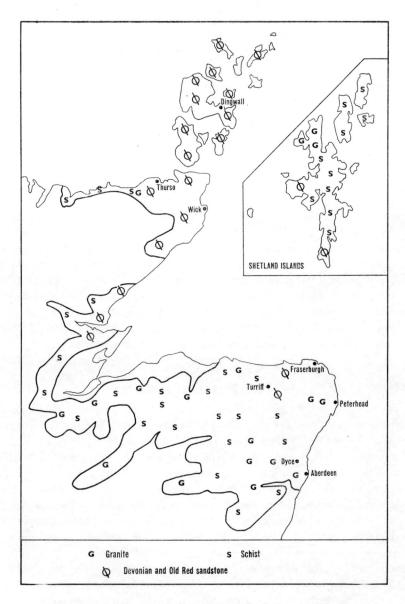

FIG. 8. The north east stock rearing and feeding areas of Scotland.

TABLE 4

SOME CLIMATIC DATA FOR NORTH EAST SCOTLAND

Station	J	F	M	A	M	J	J	A	S	O	N	D	Y
					Total rainfall (mm)								
Wick	74	51	46	52	46	52	65	67	74	79	80	75	761
Dyce	77	57	52	56	68	52	85	76	78	91	90	80	862
					Monthly mean temperature (°C)								
Wick	3·8	4·0	4·8	6·1	8·1	10·6	12·7	12·5	11·2	8·7	6·1	4·7	7·8
Dyce	2·8	3·2	4·6	6·2	8·7	11·6	13·7	13·3	11·4	8·3	5·2	3·7	7·7
				Monthly mean earth temperature at 30·5 cm (°C)									
Dyce	2·7	2·6	3·8	6·1	9·0	12·1	14·2	14·2	12·2	9·1	5·8	3·8	8·0
					Bright sunshine daily mean (hours)								
Dyce	1·72	2·72	3·73	4·79	5·75	6·29	5·04	4·88	4·32	3·27	2·15	1·46	3·84

CLIMATE

Table 4 gives some indication of the climate of this region.

The rainfall of about 760 mm per annum makes the region well suited to the production of grass. On the other hand, the high figures for late summer are indicative of hazards at harvesting and the area must be considered to be marginal for cereals. Indeed, of the cereals, oats are the only ones that could be expected to yield reasonably well, though in Caithness the lower rainfall and greater sunshine have led to the development of the distilling industry, based on barley growing. The late summer rain, on the other hand, well suits the maturation of root crops. The monthly mean temperatures, together with the mean earth temperatures, show that growth of crops can be expected to commence in late April and to continue until almost the end of October. It is noteworthy that the hours of bright sunshine are among the highest recorded in Scotland.

From the foregoing discussions it can be seen that the conditions of soil and climate together have dictated that agriculture in this region should be based on stock rearing and fattening; fattening farms are found on the better soil on the lower ground in eastern Aberdeen. The development of dairy farms around the main towns is a result of the proximity of a ready market for liquid milk sales.

THE EASTERN COASTAL STRIP AS FAR NORTH AS ABERDEEN AND INCLUDING THE LAICH OF MORAY

THIS region includes South East Berwickshire and the extreme north of Northumberland, the greater part of East Lothian, Fife, Kinross, the eastern part of Perth, Angus and Kincardine ; also included is the northern part of Moray. The dominant enterprise is cropping, and sale crops are a major source of income for over 45 per cent of the full-time farmers. Over 70 per cent of all farms of this type in Scotland are found in this region.

GEOLOGY AND SOILS

The most fertile soils in these areas are those derived from the Old Red Sandstone. This deposit can be divided into two series : the Upper and the Lower ; in some areas both series are almost equally represented, but in others one or the other predominates. The red sandstones and marls, which form highly fertile agricultural land in North Berwickshire, in Roxburghshire and in part of East Lothian, belong in the main to the Upper series. The derived soil is especially suited to potatoes, and the high fertility is in part due to the presence of basic volcanic material in these rocks, which gradually weathers to give an abundance of plant foods. Some of the soils of Tweedside and North Northumberland are derived from Boulder Clay, but the main characteristic of the area is alluvium, giving highly fertile land well suited to arable farming ; these fertile soils extend southwards along the Till River almost as far as Wooler. The well-known agricultural districts of Strathmore and the Carse of Gowrie have soils essentially similar to those of the East Lothians, though in many parts the soil is actually derived from Boulder Clay and other glacial deposits. Along the Laich of Moray the lower Old Red Sandstone strata predominate, consisting of red sandstone, conglomerates, shales and flagstones ; the soils formed in this area are again of great fertility. Almost everywhere the Old Red Sandstone series are of a nature which weathers readily to give a deep, free-working, and well-drained soil that is at once easy to cultivate and is readily penetrated by plant roots.

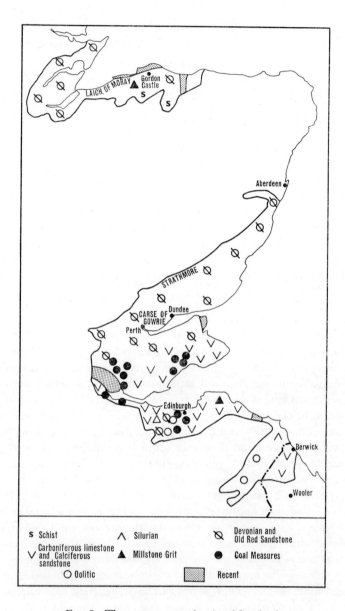

Fig. 9. The eastern coastal strip of Scotland.

TABLE 5

SOME CLIMATIC DATA FOR THE EASTERN COASTAL STRIP

Station	J	F	M	A	M	J	J	A	S	O	N	D	Y
Total rainfall (mm)													
Gordon Castle (Works)	60	47	43	46	53	57	78	79	78	80	73	57	751
Dundee (Works)	71	55	50	45	66	51	82	87	69	83	72	61	792
Edinburgh	62	43	41	41	56	48	77	80	65	72	61	54	700
Monthly mean temperature (°C)													
Gordon Castle	3·5	3·9	5·3	7·1	9·8	12·6	14·7	14·2	12·1	8·8	5·7	4·1	8·5
Dundee (Mayfield)	3·1	3·6	5·1	7·1	9·7	13·0	15·0	14·4	12·2	8·8	5·4	3·9	8·4
Edinburgh	3·7	3·8	5·2	7·0	9·5	12·7	14·7	14·2	12·3	9·1	6·0	4·5	8·6
Monthly mean earth temperature at 30·5 cm (°C)													
Dundee (Mayfield)	2·4	2·6	4·2	7·1	10·4	13·9	15·8	15·4	13·1	9·4	5·4	3·4	8·6
Edinburgh	3·1	3·3	4·6	7·1	10·3	13·7	15·4	14·9	12·8	9·4	5·7	4·1	8·7
Bright sunshine daily mean (hours)													
Gordon Castle	1·47	2·51	3·58	4·46	5·57	5·71	4·67	4·62	3·83	2·96	1·76	1·09	3·52
Dundee (Mayfield)	1·61	2·69	3·39	4·65	5·36	6·08	4·97	4·55	4·06	3·07	2·10	1·32	3·65
Edinburgh	1·69	2·68	3·69	4·62	5·55	6·52	5·20	4·62	4·24	3·21	2·08	1·46	3·80

CLIMATE

Table 5 illustrates the climatic conditions of this region. The comparatively dry spring is one of the more notable factors ; this enables the spring work associated with arable farming to be started early and completed in ample time to make full use of the growing season. The growing season in these areas commences towards the end of March and continues until well into November. The summer days are long and this makes a major contribution to the ripening of crops, especially cereals. The high rainfall in July and August—in all of the examples two of the wettest months of the year—tends to reduce the quality of barley, a crop that would prefer a high rainfall in June followed by a dry July and August.

The intensive farming associated with this region of Scotland is somewhat surprising in view of its occurrence as far north as latitudes 57°–59° N. The high fertility of the area is the result of the interaction of several factors : (a) the inherent nature of the rocks and the presence of drift material which contributes materials of varying composition to the soil ; (b) the comparatively low elevation ; (c) the climate. It is not possible to say which of these factors is the most important, but it is pertinent that the Torridon Sandstone of the west coast of Scotland gives plateaux covered with heather and peat, which are hardly cultivated. This area is at a similar latitude to the fertile east coast soils and the Torridon Sandstone is lithologically similar to the Old Red Sandstone—a striking example of the influence of elevation and climate.

CHAPTER 3

THE CENTRAL LOWLANDS

THE demarcation of this area to the north is the Highland Boundary Fault and that to the south is the Southern Upland Fault ; to the east the boundary can be taken as the junction with the east coast arable strip and to the west the boundary is the coast line. Thus much of Dumbarton, Stirling, Renfrewshire, and the northern parts of Ayrshire and Lanarkshire are included. Most of the area lies in the Midland Valley of Scotland and the main farming enterprise is dairying.

GEOLOGY AND SOILS

The Midland Valley comprises three units : the Helensburgh–Stonehaven trough to the north, the lava hills which confine the valley to the south, and the dominantly carboniferous lowlands. The carboniferous lowlands are devoted almost exclusively to dairying ; the rocks of the system consist in the main of limestones, sandstones, shales, coal seams, and harder volcanic rocks. The volcanic rocks form ranges of hills such as the Kilpatrick Hills and the Campsie Fells. Glaciation has contributed to the diversity of the region with Boulder Clay deposits, glacial tills of various textures, moraines, and fluvioglacial sands and gravels. Marine alluvium and accumulations of hill and basin peats also occur together with raised beaches of sands, gravels, silts and clays. A notable feature is the raised beach between Alloway and Troon. An important superficial deposit is dune sand on the seaward side of the raised beach from Prestwick northwards. This area together with the alluvial soils of Ayr is characterized by light freely drained soils, ideally suited for early potatoes. Some market gardening is found around Ayr. In the vicinity of Maybole, the hills are mainly derived from Lower Old Red Sandstone and again the associated land is of high fertility. Farther north and away from the coast, most of the soils are poorly drained and often overlie a tenacious Boulder Clay. Almost without exception these soils are of low fertility. The major soil groups represented in this area are Podzols, Brown Forest soils of low base status, Low humic-gley soils, and Peaty gley soils.

CLIMATE

Reference to Table 6 shows that this area is characterized by high rainfall and low sunshine, but that the temperatures are mild. The differences between Stirling and Paisley illustrate the general differences in climate observed as one progresses westwards. Further emphasis of these differences can be obtained

81

by comparing these figures with those given for Edinburgh in Table 5. The heavy rainfall makes for good pasture, but renders most of the area unsuitable for extensive cash cropping. The exception here is the coastal strip, and the town of Ayr, with its local market, has led to the development of horticulture on the fertile soils around it.

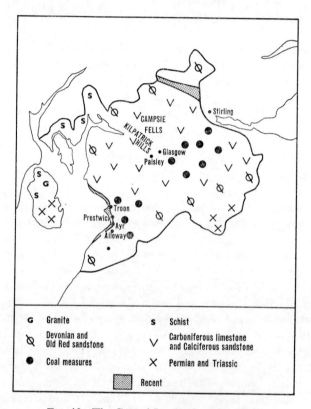

FIG. 10. The Central Lowlands of Scotland.

It can be seen therefore that the system of farming followed in this region is the result of the interaction of three factors :

(a) The densely populated industrial region round Glasgow and along the Clyde.

(b) The climate and in particular the high rainfall.

(c) The soil type.

The dominant factor is probably the demand for liquid milk in the industrial areas, and this in itself would have lead to an emphasis on dairy farming ; but in this region this influence is undoubtedly supported by both the climate and the soil.

TABLE 6

SOME CLIMATIC DATA FOR THE CENTRAL LOWLANDS

Station	J	F	M	A	M	J	J	A	S	O	N	D	Y
Total rainfall (mm)													
Stirling	116	73	59	55	66	57	80	88	87	106	96	96	979
Paisley	132	88	71	63	71	65	83	91	98	130	113	117	1122
Monthly mean temperature (°C)													
Stirling	3·4	4·1	5·6	7·7	10·4	13·6	15·3	14·8	12·4	9·1	5·6	4·2	8·9
Paisley	4·0	4·4	5·9	8·0	10·9	13·9	15·6	15·1	12·7	9·5	6·2	4·7	9·2
Monthly mean earth temperature at 30·5 cm (°C)													
Stirling	3·0	2·8	4·2	7·2	10·8	14·6	16·2	15·6	13·0	9·4	5·6	3·9	8·9
Paisley	3·7	3·8	5·1	7·9	11·2	14·6	16·2	15·7	13·3	9·9	6·4	4·7	9·4
Bright sunshine daily mean (hours)													
Stirling	1·03	2·07	3·27	4·42	5·06	5·81	4·42	4·16	3·75	2·55	1·66	0·93	3·26
Paisley	0·93	1·85	2·93	4·50	5·56	6·08	4·90	4·47	3·79	2·41	1·39	0·80	3·30

CHAPTER 4

SOUTH WEST SCOTLAND

SOUTH WEST SCOTLAND has much in common with the Central Lowlands described in the previous chapter. Included in this region are Wigtownshire, Kirkcudbright, Dumfriesshire and Southern Ayrshire. The farming is characterized by two main enterprises—dairying and hill sheep farming; this is a rather unusual combination and nowhere in Great Britain, with the possible exception of the Dales of Northern England, is it so clearly developed.

GEOLOGY AND SOILS

The region includes the south western part of the Southern Uplands with summits of over 760 m and some very rugged ground falling to rounded grassy hill in Dumfries and to moors in Kirkcudbright, Wigtownshire and Southern Ayrshire. The lower lying ground is mainly found along the coast and along the valleys of the rivers. The majority of the region is underlain by Ordovician and Silurian rocks, but the parent material of the soil is mainly glacial tills derived from various materials such as greywackes, sandstones, shales, basic lavas and other basic and acid igneous rocks. Fluvioglacial deposits, moraines and drumlins are all found. The extensive raised beaches on the coastal strip as far south as the Mull of Galloway are characterized by light freely drained soils, ideally suited for early potatoes. Farther inland the soils are somewhat heavier and on the whole poorly drained. On the other hand, the soils on the north coast of the Solway Firth are generally fertile and support dairy farming with important arable enterprises.

CLIMATE

Table 7 gives some indication of the climate. It has already been noted that this region has some similarities with the Midland Valley, and a comparison with Table 6 will emphasize this point, particularly in relation to sunshine and temperatures. The rainfall is suited to the production of grass, potatoes, and other root crops, but is rather too high for other arable crops and particularly for cereals. Farther inland and on higher ground the rainfall increases dramatically: thus at Moffat, less than 32 km north of Ruthwell, but at 145 m as compared with 29 m, the annual rainfall is over 1450 mm.

84

It is interesting that, though this region is relatively remote from the densely populated industrial region of Clydeside, the emphasis on lower lying farms is nevertheless on dairying. This is largely the result of the combination of soil and climate which gave rise to the farmhouse cheese industry, at one time the most profitable outlet for quality grass production. With the coming of transport facilities for milk through the M.M.B., the farmhouse cheese industry has given

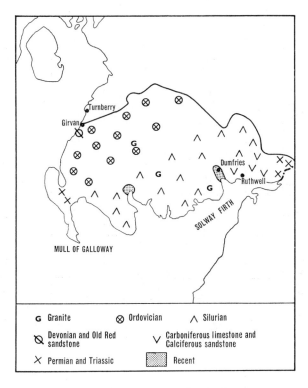

FIG. 11. South West Scotland.

way to sales of liquid milk. A combination of high land and low land on farms gave rise to the association of dairy and hill sheep. The light sandy soils of the coast, in an area relatively free from frost and with adequate rainfall, has made this area famous for early potatoes. More surprising is the dominance of arable farming along the Solway, where rainfall is so high as to preclude many other areas from a system of farming based on sale crops; this is undoubtedly the result of light free draining soils in an area of moderate sunshine and warmth. On the poorer grasslands of the higher districts stock rearing is the dominant enterprise.

TABLE 7

SOME CLIMATIC DATA FOR THE SOUTH WEST OF SCOTLAND

Station	J	F	M	A	M	J	J	A	S	O	N	D	Y
Total rainfall (mm)													
Girvan	126	75	69	60	68	69	87	94	104	127	116	123	1118
Ruthwell (Comlongen Castle)	99	59	58	51	59	64	87	100	84	100	86	88	935
Monthly mean temperature (°C)													
Turnberry	4·7	4·7	6·1	7·9	10·4	12·9	14·7	14·4	12·9	10·1	7·0	5·5	9·3
Ruthwell	3·1	3·6	5·3	7·3	10·5	13·4	15·1	14·7	12·4	9·1	5·5	3·7	8·6
Monthly mean earth temperature at 30·5 cm (°C)													
Dumfries	3·8	3·7	4·9	7·4	10·6	13·9	15·5	15·4	13·6	10·4	6·8	4·9	9·2
Bright sunshine daily mean (hours)													
Turnberry	1·26	2·37	3·62	5·17	6·60	6·53	5·02	4·83	3·94	2·69	1·73	1·13	3·74
Dumfries	1·29	2·21	3·34	4·56	5·95	6·39	4·86	4·58	3·73	2·84	1·86	1·13	3·56

THE NORTH WEST AND CENTRAL HIGHLANDS

By far the greater part of Scotland is land that is too high for any intensive agriculture and is devoted to rearing hill sheep or to deer forests. This includes much of Caithness, Sutherland, Ross and Cromarty, Inverness, Perthshire, and Argyllshire. In these areas, on the lower ground, where the soil is deeper and somewhat less infertile, and where the climate is kinder, a system of farming, peculiar to Scotland, developed ; this system is known as crofting.

GEOLOGY AND SOILS

The greater part of the area is underlain by a series of rocks known as the Highland Schists ; also included are felspathic gneisses, quartzites, slates, and crystalline limestone. The oldest rocks are mainly metamorphosed igneous rocks, but some of the younger ones are sedimentary in origin. For the most part rainfall is extremely high and erosion has kept pace with soil formation ; the naked rock has given an overall sterile appearance to the area, but at the same time it is a region of great scenic beauty. Some of the rocks could be expected to yield fertile soils under more favourable climatic conditions ; an example of such a rock is the Torridon Sandstone, similar in many respects to the Old Red Sandstone, though somewhat harder. It has already been noted that on the east coast of Scotland, where the rainfall is less, the Old Red Sandstone gives some highly fertile soils ; in the west of Scotland the Torridon Sandstone is a mountainous area with some of the most remarkable peaks in the British Isles.

CLIMATE

Two factors contribute to the bleakness of the Highlands : elevation and climate. Almost all of the region has a rainfall of over 1300 mm per annum and in many places records of 2500 mm or more are obtained. Even with stations at low elevations high rainfalls are recorded: at Lochgoilhead the annual rainfall is 2290 mm and the height of the station is 6·1 m ; the high rainfall here is the result of the surrounding peaks. At Oban the annual rainfall is nearly 1450 mm—partly owing to the high ground of Mull, but dominantly the result of the prevailing westerly wind. The high rainfall is associated with a low value for average bright sunshine ; for the greater part of the region the mean is less than 3·3 hours per day.

It can be seen therefore that even the cropping areas in the valleys are subject to high rainfall. The winters are less severe than those experienced on the east

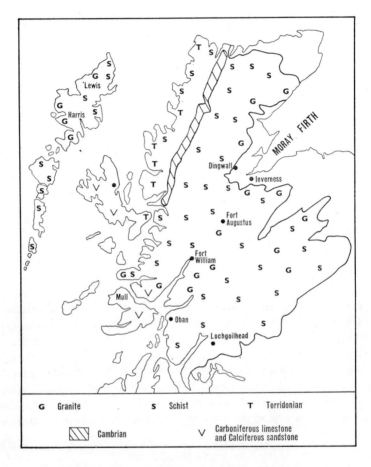

Fig. 12. The North West and Central Highlands.

coast but the summers are very much colder than those experienced in the south. Cropping is therefore severely restricted and the only crop that is of any importance is oats.

CROFTING

Crofting was a system of part-time farming whereby some of the family worked on a small area of land and some devoted their time to other occupations—

often fishing. The croft consisted of 1–4 hectares carrying one or two cows and a few sheep. The climate of the area is certainly suited for growing fodder for livestock and a varied selection of vegetables for human consumption, but the croft itself could not support a family. With the decline in the prosperity of inshore fishing, crofting itself has declined and is today of much less economic significance than 30 years ago. Some crofts survive, however ; in some cases two or three crofts have been amalgamated into one unit of a size more capable of supporting a family ; in other cases the income of the croft is supplemented by catering for the tourist traffic of the Highlands ; in still other cases forestry has replaced fishing as the supplementary occupation of the crofter. Some crofts have been amalgamated into existing large holdings and the land that was once cultivated has reverted to sheep walks.

CHAPTER 6

THE BORDER COUNTRY

THIS region includes the southern part of Lanarkshire, Peeblesshire, Selkirkshire, the south of Midlothian, the west of Berwickshire, Roxburghshire, a small part

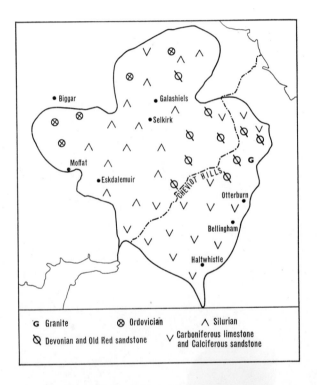

FIG. 13. The Border Country.

of East Dumfriesshire, and extends into Central Northumberland as far south as Haltwhistle and including the north east of Cumberland. The enterprises that dominate the farming of this region are stock rearing and hill sheep farming.

TABLE 8

SOME CLIMATIC DATA FOR THE BORDERS

Station	J	F	M	A	M	J	J	A	S	O	N	D	Y
Total rainfall (mm)													
Eskdalemuir	192	117	101	97	96	101	127	140	140	166	152	159	1588
Galashiels	99	68	61	55	66	54	76	88	75	99	87	86	914
Monthly mean temperature (°C)													
Eskdalemuir	2·0	2·1	3·6	5·6	8·6	11·4	13·3	12·8	10·5	7·4	4·2	2·7	7·0
Bellingham	1·7	2·1	4·0	6·0	9·1	12·1	13·9	13·3	11·1	7·8	4·3	2·5	7·3
Monthly mean earth temperature at 30·5 cm (°C)													
Eskdalemuir	3·5	3·2	4·1	6·5	9·5	12·4	14·2	14·4	12·7	9·3	6·8	4·8	8·5
Bright sunshine daily mean (hours)													
Eskdalemuir	1·19	2·14	3·11	4·20	5·40	5·72	4·43	4·02	3·32	2·58	1·79	1·15	3·25

GEOLOGY AND SOILS

The underlying rocks are mainly Silurian Shales, but on the borders there is an area of Carboniferous Calciferous Sandstone and, farther south, Carboniferous Limestone. The Cheviot Hills comprise a central core of Cheviot Granite surrounded by Andesite Lava formations of lower Old Red Sandstone age. Most of the higher ground is covered by short grass with some heather and here the land is devoted to sheep rearing, which has given rise to a considerable wool industry with centres at Galashiels, Selkirk, and Otterburn. The soils consist dominantly of podzolic and peaty soils with some hill peat ; immature soils with humose rock rubble over a brown sand are also found. On lower lying ground Brown Forest soils of low base status or with gleyed B or C horizons support some mixed arable farming and stock rearing.

CLIMATE

Some indication of the climate of this region is given in Table 8. In interpreting these data, differences in altitude should be noted : Eskdalemuir is at 242 m and Galashiels is at 137 m; Bellingham, in Northumberland, is at 260 m. The region is characterized by high rainfalls and a short growing season. Grass cannot be expected to commence growth until well into April and in most years it is late May before there is sufficient growth to support lactating ewes.

The agriculture of the Border Country is mainly governed by topography and climate, both of which have had their effect on soil formation. Thus above 305m all the soils are leached and occur under a severe climate of high winds, high rainfall, and low temperatures. Hill sheep farming is the only possible enterprise. On lower lying ground some arable farming and stock rearing is practised, especially to the east of the region where the climate is less rigorous, and, as a result of this, the soils are of higher fertility ; such areas occur in the Tweed, Leader, and Gala Valleys.

BIBLIOGRAPHY

CENTRAL OFFICE OF INFORMATION. *Agriculture in Britain.* H.M.S.O. (1961).
DARLING, F. F. *Crofting Agriculture: Its Practice in the West Highlands and Islands.* Oliver and Boyd (1945).
DEPARTMENT OF AGRICULTURE FOR SCOTLAND. *Agriculture in Scotland.* H.M.S.O. (1955).
DEPARTMENT OF AGRICULTURE FOR SCOTLAND. *Scotland's Marginal Farms.* H.M.S.O. (1947).
DEPARTMENT OF AGRICULTURE FOR SCOTLAND. *Types of Farming in Scotland.* H.M.S.O. (1952).
MERCER, W. (ed.). *British Farming.* H.M.S.O. (1951).
PAWSON, H. C. *A Survey of the Agriculture of Northumberland.* R.A.S.E. (1962).
SANDERS, H. G. and ELEY, C. *Farms of Britain.* Crosby and Lockwood (1946).

Agricultural Regions of England and Wales

INTRODUCTION

ON THE basis of the farming systems, it has been possible to divide Scotland into six regions. An examination of a map showing the types of farming found in Great Britain (Fig. 15) will reveal the logic of such a division. In the case of

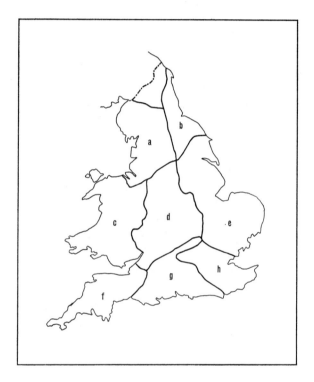

FIG. 14. Farming regions of England and Wales.

England and Wales, however, a much greater diversity of farming systems will be noted ; indeed it is probable that nowhere else in the world is there an area of land of comparable size that supports so many different systems of farming. This is undoubtedly the result of a complex geological structure associated with considerable variations both in relief and in climate. It is not therefore possible

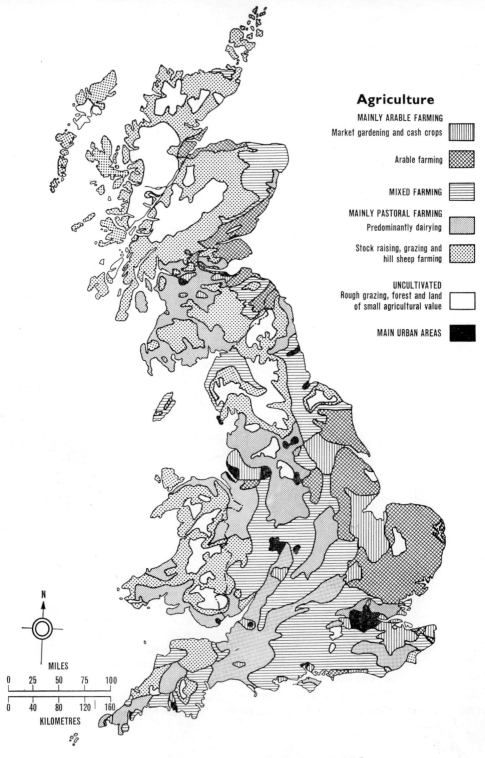

Agriculture

MAINLY ARABLE FARMING

Market gardening and cash crops

Arable farming

MIXED FARMING

MAINLY PASTORAL FARMING

Predominantly dairying

Stock raising, grazing and
hill sheep farming

UNCULTIVATED

Rough grazing, forest and land
of small agricultural value

MAIN URBAN AREAS

N

MILES

| 0 | 25 | 50 | 75 | 100 |

| 0 | 40 | 80 | 120 | 160 |

KILOMETRES

Fig. 15. Farming types in Great Britain.
(Reproduction from *Agriculture in Britain*, H.M.S.O.)

to regionalize England and Wales on an agricultural basis without making the number of regions inordinately large. Nevertheless, it is convenient to consider the agriculture on a regional basis, but it should be noted that these regions are fundamentally geographical rather than agricultural ; consequently in many cases, the region will often include a number of widely differing agricultural systems and in some instances the region will be subdivided. The agriculture of England and Wales will be considered under the following headings (see Fig. 14) :

(a) The North West of England, the Lake District and the Pennines.
(b) The North East of England.
(c) Wales and the Welsh Borders.
(d) Central England.
(e) Eastern England.
(f) South West England.
(g) Central Southern England.
(h) South East England.

CHAPTER 1

THE NORTH WEST OF ENGLAND, THE LAKE DISTRICT AND THE PENNINES

THIS region consists of Cumberland, Westmorland, Lancashire and Cheshire, together with the Pennine districts of West Durham, the North and West Ridings of Yorkshire, and Derbyshire. In this region there are three fairly well-defined districts :

(a) The hill farming areas of the Lake District and the Pennines.

(b) The low ground of the Eden Valley and around Carlisle.

(c) The Plain of Lancastria.

GEOLOGY AND SOILS

The geological pattern of the Lake District may be said to run approximately ENE–WSW. To the north of a line from Troutbeck to Egremont are found the Skiddaw slates of the Ordovician system, and to the south of a line from Shap Wells to Millom occur various grits, sandy flags, and slates of the Silurian system. Between these two lines are the green, grey and purple lavas and volcanic ashes of the Borrowdale Volcanic Series, again of Ordovician age. These masses of ancient rocks in the heart of the Lake District are surrounded by younger rocks dipping away from the central core. On the coast, south of St. Bees Head, the under-lying rocks are Keuper and Bunter Sandstones (Triassic New Red Sandstone). Between St. Bees Head and Maryport are productive Coal Measures with some outcrops of Millstone Grit. To the north and east of the Lake District are Carboniferous Limestone, Permian New Red Sandstone and Keuper Marl.

To the south west of the rocks of the Lake District lie the Carboniferous Limestone and Millstone Grit of the Pennines. In the Plain of Lancastria there are two broad tongues of moorland running westwards from the Pennines, which again coincide with outcrops of Millstone Grit and also of the Lower Coal Measures. The majority of this plain, however, is undulating lowland : there are low hills where Bunter Sandstone outcrops and true lowland where Keuper Marl is the underlying rock.

101

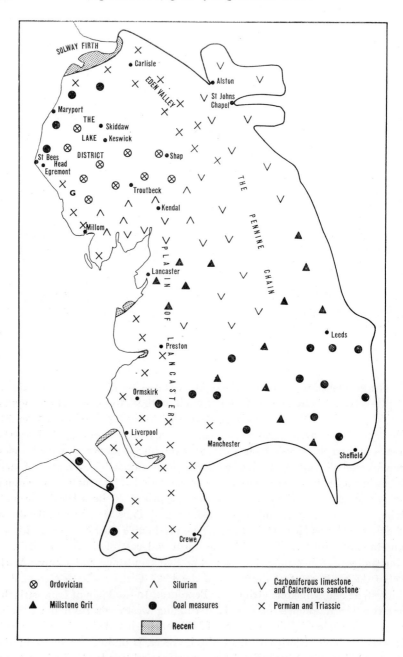

FIG. 16. The North West of England.

THE LAKE DISTRICT

The high ground of the region is partly covered by thin, skeletal soils, strewn with boulders ; in many places the rocks are bare. In the valleys the soil is more plentiful and most farmsteads, in the Lake District for example, are situated on this better land with access to fell grazings. Sheep provide the greater part of the farming income in the Lake District and Pennines and there are three main breeds to be found : on the poorest hills in the west the Herdwick, the hardiest of all breeds in the British Isles, is still dominant ; on the other hand, wherever conditions are less exacting this breed has largely been replaced by the Swaledale. To the north and east of Kendal is the home of the Rough Fell, but this breed is numerically of less importance than the Herdwick. Milk production has increased steadily over the past twenty years though stock rearing is still important. Milk costs are high as a result of the long winter and the shortage of spring grass : what grass there is will often be required by the ewes, between lambing and when they return to the hill. In some districts suckler cows have replaced the dairy stock, but the typically small size of these farms (between 20 and 40 hectares) limits the number of stock that can be carried; furthermore, most of the profit from suckler cows in this district comes from the hill cow and calf subsidies and the advisability of a change to suckler cows is therefore questionable. It is interesting that the trend over the past forty years has been towards fewer farms and larger holdings.

THE PENNINES

To the east of the Lake District lie the Pennines. In some of this area soil derived from glacial till is found ; in other parts the Carboniferous Limestone has given rise to Karst scenery : such scenery is found where the limestone forms a level area, free from drift, and the surface consists of bare rock with fissures, called " grikes ", in which vegetation grows. Where soil is found on the limestone, the vegetation is dominantly agrostis-fescue turf ; where drift occurs to some depth peat may be formed. The Millstone Grit of the Pennines gives rise to open moorland, which is peaty and covered with heather. As with the Lake District, sheep are the dominant enterprise with a limited number of beef cattle on the lower ground and some concentration of dairy farming in the valleys : dairy farming is found especially in the valleys of the eastern slopes of the Pennines and to the south.

Much of the low-lying ground to the west of the Lake District is marginal ; the soils here are derived dominantly from Boulder Clay and are heavy, cold and wet. This land is best suited to grass, and milk is the main source of income. Most of the farms extend to about 40 hectares. Sheep are also important with *draft ewes* from the hills being crossed with Border Leicester or the Teeswater rams. The *gimmer lambs* from this cross are often sold for breeding to farms on

H

the fertile land of the Solway coast, but the *wethers* are fattened on rape. The soils along the Solway coast are mainly derived from either blown sand or alluvium. Such soils are light in texture, friable and fertile ; they are usually deep and are often red in colour. This area is one of mixed farming with cropping governed by the requirements of livestock production, though a particularly interesting crop is peas grown for canning in Maryport. Oats grow well, often yielding 5 tonnes to the hectare, and there is a fairly large quantity of roots.

THE EDEN VALLEY

The Eden Valley is again fertile with a soil mainly derived from till of the New Red Sandstone. Being on the lee side of the mountains this area has a lower rainfall, in some places less than 760 mm; there is therefore considerable emphasis on arable farming coupled with stock rearing and feeding. Dairy farming is relatively unimportant.

THE PLAIN OF LANCASTRIA

The Plain of Lancastria is largely covered by complex glacial drift giving rise to a wide range of different textured soils. Brown Forest soils, Podzolic soils, Gley soils, and Organic soils are all represented. Here are also found deposits of glacial sands and gravels, fluvioglacial gravel, sands and gravels of morainic complexes and alluvium. Where the soils are derived from the underlying Keuper Marl, they are heavy, whereas where they are derived from the Bunter Sandstone they are light. In the Ormskirk region sandy soils with humose or peaty sand surface horizons overlying bleached sand have given some of the most fertile land in the country ; here there is an almost complete absence of permanent grass and this is the only major area in the west of England where wheat is an important crop. The area of potatoes is especially large, and stock farming is relatively unimportant. To the north and to the south of the Ormskirk area the soils are generally heavier and are mainly under grass ; the dominant enterprise here is dairy farming, though both pigs and poultry are important.

CLIMATE

Table 9 gives some climatic data for this region. Keswick is taken as the station for the Lake District and it will be noted that a rainfall of nearly 1525 mm per annum is recorded. But the Keswick station is at only 77 metres and on the higher ground of the district rainfalls of over 2500 mm have been recorded; 2000–2500 mm is normal. To the west of the high ground of the Lake District and along the Solway coast 750–1000 mm may be taken as average. The monthly earth temperatures show that Hutton has the longest growing season, though winter temperatures fall below those of Keswick.

TABLE 9

SOME CLIMATIC DATA FOR THE NORTH WEST OF ENGLAND

Station	J	F	M	A	M	J	J	A	S	O	N	D	Y
Total rainfall (mm)													
Keswick	170	107	87	83	81	82	111	128	142	172	155	153	1471
Penrith	151	95	76	72	66	65	87	106	108	139	128	128	1221
Hutton (Preston)	88	63	51	51	62	64	85	99	94	100	94	84	935
Monthly mean temperature (°C)													
Keswick	4·2	4·2	5·8	7·6	10·6	13·4	15·3	14·9	12·7	9·7	6·4	4·8	9·1
Newton Rigg	2·9	3·2	4·8	7·0	10·1	12·9	14·7	14·2	11·9	8·6	5·2	3·5	8·3
Hutton	3·8	4·2	5·8	8·0	10·9	13·8	15·6	15·4	13·3	9·3	6·3	4·5	9·2
Monthly mean earth temperature at 30·5 cm (°C)													
Keswick	4·1	3·9	4·8	7·4	10·7	14·2	15·7	15·7	13·7	10·6	7·2	5·1	9·4
Hutton	3·8	3·7	4·9	7·8	11·1	14·4	16·1	15·8	13·9	10·7	7·0	4·8	9·5
Bright sunshine daily mean (hours)													
Keswick	1·03	1·89	3·26	4·43	5·88	6·08	4·64	4·39	3·47	2·33	1·39	0·83	3·30
Newton Rigg	1·28	2.22	3·44	4·55	5·94	6·31	5·03	4·74	3·77	2·75	1·73	1·06	3·57
Hutton	1·05	1·92	3·24	4·82	6·00	6·36	5·07	4·96	3·91	2·68	1·47	0·88	3·53

In the Lake District and on the Pennines the choice of a farming enterprise is limited by topography, which in turn is associated with an adverse climate and poor soils. The influence of the tourist traffic has led to some specialization in dairying in the valleys, where conditions are less exacting. On the eastern slopes of the Pennines in the valleys of Weardale and Teesdale the development of the dairy industry was to some extent associated with the demand of the industrial east coast.

On the Southern Pennines in East Lancashire and in Derbyshire the effect of industrialization is still more clearly shown. Many of the farmers are producer-retailers, thus perpetuating a system considered to be outdated by many modern agriculturists. Whilst the soil is not always well suited to dairy farming, the climate is conducive to good grassland and high milk yields are achieved. Industrial pollution may in some cases reduce the incidence of some plant diseases such as potato blight. But the proximity of a large market is not without its disadvantages : industrial pollution has a deleterious effect on soil fertility, the health of animals, and the life of machines, buildings, and fences ; much damage results from trespass, and sheep farming is virtually ruled out by marauding dogs. In consequence sheep are restricted to the Nardus and Molinia rough grazings of the hills ; here is the home of the Derbyshire Gritstone. The area around Manchester probably has the highest concentration of pigs in the country, and the availability of urban swill has lead to pigs being fed on a factory scale.

Dairy farming in the areas to the north and south of the Ormskirk area in the Plain of Lancastria is the result of industrialization coupled with suitable conditions of soil and climate. In the Ormskirk region itself, soil conditions have encouraged the development of a more intensive farming system very similar to that found in the Fens of eastern England.

CHAPTER 2

THE NORTH EAST OF ENGLAND

THIS region comprises the area running south and east from the Border Country to a line drawn approximately from Filey to Leeds ; the region is bounded on the west by the Pennines and on the east by the coast. Thus the eastern parts of Northumberland and Durham, the North and West Ridings of Yorkshire and the northern part of the East Riding of Yorkshire are all included.

GEOLOGY AND SOILS

The underlying rock in the north is Carboniferous Limestone. South and east of the Carboniferous Limestone are the productive Coal Measures, occupying a tract of land running approximately ENE–SSW between two lines one drawn from Amble to Slaley and the other from South Shields to West Auckland. Between the Coal Measures and the Carboniferous Limestone a narrow strip of Millstone Grit is found. The Magnesian Limestone runs approximately SSE from the coast between South Shields and Hartlepool, inland as far as Staindrop and then south in a belt mainly between three and five miles wide as far as Nottingham. To the south and east of the Magnesian Limestone are found Bunter Sandstone, Keuper Marl, and Lias ; the Cleveland Hills are mainly Oolitic and the Vale of Pickering, marking part of the southern boundary of the region, is a vast alluvial deposit.

The majority of the region is drift covered, and only in limited areas are the soils formed directly from the underlying strata. Carboniferous drift, the most common parent material, varies in texture from light loam to clay and the associated soils are correspondingly variable.

In the north of Northumberland in an area mainly to the east of the Great North Road the soils are red-brown and vary in texture from loams to clay loams ; in the extreme north there is some admixture of Old Red Sandstone till. Here are found some of the finest fattening pastures in the country—somewhat surprising in view of the low rainfall ; but the soil holds moisture, and with good management the better species of grasses remain dominant in the sward ; the response to phosphate applications is striking and the regular use of basic slag has done much to maintain the productivity of the pastures. The high quality of the grassland is a tribute to the work of Somerville, Middleton, and Gilchrist, of Cockle Park. In some districts, arable cropping is important and wheat is the corn crop best suited to the soil.

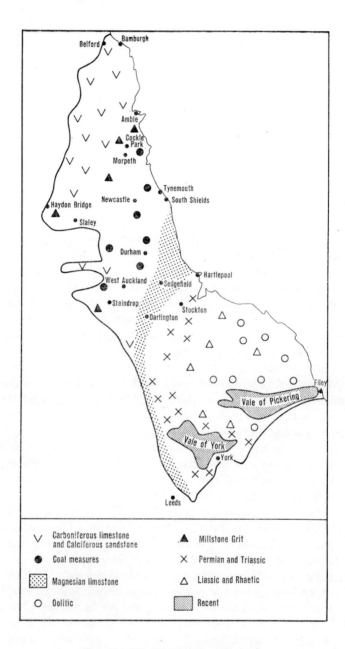

Fig. 17. The North East of England.

To the west of the Great North Road and north of Morpeth some of the soils are associated with either Cementstone or Fell Sandstone (of the lower Carboniferous strata). Those derived from drift of Cementstone, usually with an admixture of Andesite Lava, are brown medium or light loams ; small outcrops of Cementstone give well-drained soils. Soils derived from the Fell sandstone are very poor, generally stony and podzolized.

Farther south, towards Tynemouth and east of the Great North Road, heavier soils become more common, though there are several areas of sand and gravel giving a lighter soil ; indeed in exceptional seasons there are some soils that are liable to wind erosion. Such lighter soils are generally in shorter arable rotations. In South Northumberland and west of the Great North Road from Newcastle to Morpeth there are some good quality soils, again mainly derived from Carboniferous till, and varying in texture from loam to clay loam. Along the Tyne Valley and as far west as Haydon Bridge there are alluvial sands and gravels that give rise to some of the best agricultural soils in Northumberland.

Magnesian limestone sedentary soils cover a considerable area in East Durham, though there is usually some admixture of Boulder Clay, again of Carboniferous origin. In the west of Durham some soils derived from Carboniferous Sandstone are found, as also are patches of glacial sands and gravels. Heavier soils are again found in the south of Durham, especially between Darlington, Sedgefield, and Stockton, where bare fallowing is still adopted on some farms. To the west of Sedgefield there is an area of peat land, which when cultivated will grow good crops ; for the most part, however, such land is devoted to rough grazing. As with the Tyne Valley, fertile alluvium is found in the Tees Valley and, to a less extent, in the Wear Valley.

The Cleveland Hills and the North York Moors form a plateau deeply dissected by valleys. Many of the soils on the hills are sedentary rendzinas covered by rough grazing and moorland. There is little arable land, even in the valleys, partly because of the steepness of the slopes and partly because of the liability to flooding. An area of mixed farming, often based on arable production, coincides with the more fertile recent deposits of the Vale of Pickering.

The northern part of the Vale of York, lying between the North York Moors and the Pennines, and extending north towards the Tees, has also been included. This area is very complex with lacustrine, glacial, fluvioglacial, and alluvial deposits, together with outcrops of Keuper Marl, Chalk and Lias Clay, all occurring in close proximity to one another. Brown Forest soils, Podzolic soils, Peaty gleys, Gleys and Rendzinas are all found. Most of the soils are fertile and regularly cultivated, wheat, oats, barley, sugar beet, mangolds, potatoes, and carrots being the most important crops. Some of the heavier soils on the lacustrine clay are devoted to permanent grassland, the extreme flatness of the terrain making drainage difficult and flooding a real danger.

TABLE 10

SOME CLIMATIC DATA FOR THE NORTH EAST OF ENGLAND

Station	J	F	M	A	M	J	J	A	S	O	N	D	Y
Total rainfall (mm)													
Cockle Park	71	48	46	49	56	45	73	76	62	68	70	64	728
Durham	59	45	42	43	51	46	71	69	60	61	63	58	668
York	58	43	36	43	50	47	63	65	53	56	60	52	626
Monthly mean temperature (°C)													
Cockle Park	3·1	3·3	4·8	6·7	9·2	12·4	14·6	14·0	12·1	8·8	5·5	3·8	8·2
Durham	3·2	3·5	5·2	7·2	9·8	13·1	15·3	14·7	12·6	9·2	5·8	4·0	8·6
York	3·8	4·2	6·0	8·3	11·3	14·5	16·6	16·0	13·7	10·1	6·3	4·4	9·6
Monthly mean earth temperature at 30·5 cm (°C)													
York	4·0	3·9	4·9	7·6	10·8	14·0	15·8	15·8	14·0	10·8	7·3	5·0	9·5
Bright sunshine daily mean (hours)													
Cockle Park	1·62	2·43	3·48	4·69	5·52	6·23	5·26	4·66	4·20	3·19	2·19	1·53	3·75
Durham	1·54	2·31	3·35	4·52	5·27	6·04	5·11	4·75	4·03	3·09	2·04	1·44	3·62
York	1·10	1·98	3·23	4·57	5·62	6·27	5·55	5·05	4·03	2·88	1·65	1·05	3·58

CLIMATE

Some climatic data for this region are presented in Table 10. As would be expected, rainfall decreases and temperature increases from north to south. The growing season extends from late March until well into November; and in some seasons it is possible to graze dairy cattle almost until Christmas. Typical of this region is a cold dry spring which, though it may facilitate spring work on the farm, will often lead to late growth of spring grass; in some seasons grazing is not possible until May and this can lead to expensive milk production or to poor growth in lambs. August is the wettest month of the year and poor weather at harvest is commonly experienced; many farmers have therefore invested in grain drying equipment and some have recently adopted a method of storing freshly harvested wet grain in sealed silos.

AGRICULTURE

The north of this region, mainly east of the Great North Road around Belford and Bamburgh, is characterized by large farms depending mainly on fattening cattle for their income; during the Second World War there was an increase in the area of arable land with a consequent decrease in the number of cattle and sheep. In the post-war years much of this new arable land has reverted to long leys and the present-day pattern is essentially similar to that found pre-war. Skilful adjustment of stocking rates together with the exploitation of clover and basic slag have combined with favourable soil conditions to make this area one of the main centres of grass fattening in England; here is an example of soil conditions overriding the dictates of climate.

To the west of the fattening pastures the land is more variable and the agricultural systems range from dominantly sheep farming on the poorer high land to livestock and arable farming in the low land, where the soils are often light. Potatoes, sugar beet, swedes and barley are important crops; wheat is of less importance than in the east of the country. Here cross-bred sheep and suckler herds are both important.

Farther south, in the east, there is a diversity of lowland farming with dairy farming and cash cropping becoming more important towards Newcastle. To the west, the major enterprise is stock rearing except in the more fertile valleys, where mixed farming is common, and on the heavier land, where fattening pastures are again found.

The influence of industrialization on the farming system becomes more pronounced in the Wear–Tyne Lowlands and on the East Durham Plateau; here dairy farming and cash cropping with some emphasis on potatoes are the most important enterprises. Some market gardening has developed near the large towns, but adverse climatic conditions have limited the extension of this enterprise. To the west of the country, dairy farming and cash cropping gradually give way to stock rearing, but dairy farming persists on the more fertile soils of the dales, particularly in Weardale. In the southern part of the county and along the Tees Valley, the farms are usually larger than farther north, and mixed farming with more emphasis on cereal production predominates ; dairy cattle are less important, but the influence of industrialization is still shown in the large quantities of potatoes that are grown. This area of mixed farming runs southwards into the Vale of York; this is an important arable area with wheat of first importance though large areas of barley are found. The deep fertile soils favour potatoes and sugar beet ; peas and beans are found on the heavier land and carrots on the lighter. To the north east of York is an area of very light soil, where corn and sheep farming is found.

To the east of Leeds, on soils that are neither inherently fertile nor easy to cultivate, it is surprising to find a specialized horticultural industry based on rhubarb forcing, winter broccoli and, to some extent, on raspberries and strawberries. This industry must owe its origin to the proximity of the market of Leeds, presumably associated with the availability of cheap coal for heating the forcing sheds. By virtue of a low rainfall in the autumn the climatic conditions are generally favourable for lifting rhubarb for transfer to the sheds ; this also suits winter broccoli.

The North York Moors and the Cleveland Hills are of little agricultural significance and are almost entirely devoted to sheep rearing. On the lower ground, around these uplands, cattle rearing and sheep grazing are important ; in the Vale of Pickering mixed farming based on arable cropping is again found.

CHAPTER 3

WALES AND THE WELSH BORDERS

GEOLOGY AND SOILS

The Cambrian Mountains, formed mainly of Ordovician and Silurian rocks, are the dominant physical feature of Wales. In the north west the underlying rocks are mainly Ordovician and in the north east and central districts they are Silurian ; in the south west they are again Ordovician. In the central south of Wales is found the South Wales coalfield, and in the south east rocks of the Old Red Sandstone system predominate. The North Wales coalfield lies between the mountains of the north east and the Cheshire Plain. Associated with both coalfields are outcrops of Carboniferous Limestone. Small areas of Trias and Jurassic Lias Clay occur on the north and south coasts.

About 40 per cent of the total area of Wales is covered by poor siliceous soils formed from the hard sedimentary grits and sandstones of the Ordovician and Silurian systems. In some places these soils are sedentary, but in others they are formed from glacial till, itself derived from these systems. Many of the soils are podzols or peaty podzols of low fertility, but some are reasonably deep and can support limited arable enterprises ; often they are grey, acid, and deficient in phosphate ; impeded drainage may contribute to their general low fertility.

In Anglesey most of the rocks are pre-Cambrian, but, in the main, the soil is formed from Boulder Clay derived from either schists, and igneous rocks, or shales and grits of Cambrian, Ordovician, or Silurian age ; the associated soils vary in texture from heavy clays to light sandy loams ; the majority are Brown Earths, but Podzols, Gley soils and Calcareous soils have all been recognized. In Central Flintshire, on the other hand, the soils are mainly derived from Triassic Drift or from Millstone Grit and Carboniferous Limestone ; the Triassic Drift soils are the more fertile. Carboniferous Limestone soils occur elsewhere in Wales, for example in Monmouthshire, Glamorgan, and Pembrokeshire. Millstone Grit gives rise to poor sandy soils in Pembrokeshire.

Old Red Sandstone is the parent material of some highly fertile land in South Wales and also in Herefordshire. The Old Red Sandstone in these areas consists of red, brown, and yellow sandstones and conglomerates, of red marl and of beds of impure limestone called Cornstones. The sandstones and marl give rise to deep red or brown loams which are largely under permanent grass ; Herefordshire is the home of the world-famed Hereford cattle, developed on some of the finest grassland in the country. The Cornstones, as their name implies, yield a soil better suited to corn growing. On some of the higher ground, the Old Red Sandstone soils are very thin and stony ; such soils are usually derived from the conglomerates ; in Monmouthshire, for example, they vary in texture from sandy

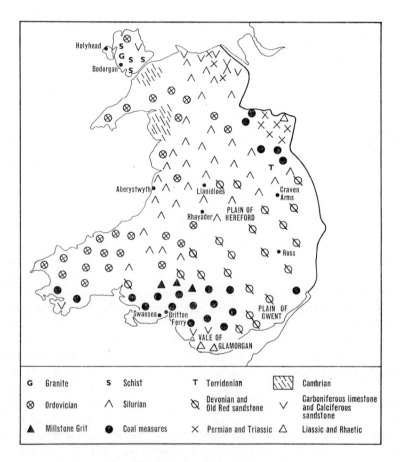

Fig. 18. Wales and the Welsh borders.

loam to silty clay loam and are much poorer than neighbouring soils derived from Carboniferous Limestone.

Alluvial deposits contribute to the complexity of the soils of Wales. Such deposits are found in most valleys and, to some extent, marine alluvium is found around the coast. The derived soils vary in texture from sandy loams to silty clays; they are sometimes calcareous, and are often fertile Brown Earths.

CLIMATE

Over the greater part of this region the dominant feature of the climate is the high rainfall. Thus even in the coastal regions rainfalls of over 1250 mm per annum are recorded. On the higher ground, farther inland, the annual rainfall is frequently between 2000 and 2500 mm, and in some areas, particularly in the north west, records of over 2500 mm are common. Still farther inland, on the Welsh borders, lower rainfalls are experienced and values of 625–900 mm are obtained. The rainfall figures generally follow the contours and rainfall, together with altitude, are important determining factors in land utilization.

AGRICULTURE OF WALES

The pattern of farming over most of Wales is very similar to that found in the Dales of the north east of England and in parts of the Lake District. It is characterized by small farms based on dairying and stock rearing. Nowhere in Great Britain did the Second World War have more effect on the farming systems. Thus in 1939 there were only 5250 hectares of wheat grown but by 1943 this crop had increased in importance to 54,000 hectares, more than a tenfold increase; this figure compares with one of just less than twofold in England over the corresponding period. The increases in the acreages of barley and oats were less dramatic and more closely followed the national trend. Since the end of the war wheat growing has declined and in the ten years ending 1957/8 the average area was 14,000 hectares, though even this is more than twice the 1939 level.

An apparently more permanent change was from dominantly stock rearing to dominantly dairying on many of the small farms in the valleys; indeed the number of cows and heifers in milk increased from 303,000 in 1945 to 367,000 in 1957—an increase of about 21 per cent; the corresponding figure for England is just over 13 per cent. This is undoubtedly largely because Welsh farming dominantly comprises small upland farms with some good land in the valleys; these farmers have found that their best chance of survival as independent units in the rather uncertain economic climate of today lies in dairying. The preponderance of small farms in Wales is illustrated by the fact that 73 per cent of all holdings are between 2 and 40 hectares, 5·75 per cent are above 60 hectares and only 0·5 per cent are over 120 hectares; the corresponding figures for England are 55 per cent, 14·1 per cent and 4·2 per cent. However, in some areas, the change of economic emphasis, which has made meat production more profitable, has combined with the high cost of alterations to buildings necessary to conform with the Milk and Dairies Regulations of 1949 to make many farmers change back to stock rearing. It is certainly true that in many cases cattle rearing fits in better than dairying on a dominantly sheep farm.

TABLE 11

SOME CLIMATIC DATA FOR WALES AND THE WELSH BORDERS

Station	J	F	M	A	M	J	J	A	S	O	N	D	Y
Total rainfall (mm)													
Bodorgan	103	68	61	53	63	64	72	86	91	113	106	102	982
Llanidloes	154	119	80	87	79	74	95	106	106	139	146	143	1328
Britton Ferry	135	92	74	72	78	74	114	117	116	139	139	133	1283
Ross-on-Wye	74	51	49	50	55	38	58	60	58	71	74	69	707
Monthly mean temperature (°C)													
Holyhead	6·1	5·8	6·8	8·4	10·7	13·3	15·1	15·3	14·0	11·4	8·6	7·0	10·2
Rhayader	3·4	3·3	4·9	7·0	9·8	12·7	14·6	14·2	12·3	8·9	5·6	4·0	8·4
Swansea	3·5	5·6	7·2	9·3	12·3	15·2	16·8	16·7	14·9	12·3	8·2	6·3	10·7
Ross-on-Wye	4·7	4·8	6·4	8·7	12·2	14·7	16·5	16·1	14·0	10·3	7·0	5·0	10·0
Monthly mean earth temperature at 30·5 cm (°C)													
Swansea	5·4	5·4	6·8	9·9	13·5	17·1	18·5	18·2	16·0	12·3	8·5	6·2	11·5
Ross-on-Wye	4·4	4·4	5·7	8·7	12·2	15·6	17·3	17·0	14·9	11·2	7·4	5·2	10·3
Bright sunshine daily mean (hours)													
Holyhead	1·77	2·65	4·04	5·81	7·07	7·39	5·98	5·65	4·63	3·28	2·00	1·30	4·30
Rhayader	1·29	2·03	3·41	4·71	5·53	6·13	5·02	4·93	3·92	2·83	1·49	1·08	3·53
Swansea	1·62	2·48	4·01	5·37	6·22	6·90	5·82	5·72	4·58	3·34	1·99	1·48	4·13
Ross-on-Wye	1·70	2·45	3·81	5·07	5·88	6·73	5·83	5·52	4·37	3·12	1·95	1·66	4·01

The preponderance of small farms has also lent impetus to reclamation in Wales; it is not surprising that the Cahn Hill Improvement Scheme at Aberystwyth should be one of the earliest of its kind in the country. An interesting development of this scheme was that small farmers in the surrounding countryside used the centre, not only for advice regarding reclamation, but also for facilities to carry out the work, including the contract hire of machinery and of labour. A similar development took place at the Grassland Station of Mixon Hay in North Staffordshire, and experience at both these centres suggests that the concept of a central development authority for marginal farms could have a wide application. It appears that such an organization, with centres at strategic locations throughout the marginal and hill lands of the country, could make a real contribution to the expansion of livestock farming in these areas. There is ample evidence that not only sheep and cattle, but also pigs and poultry, do extremely well at these higher elevations. It can be argued that the expansion of dairy farming on the marginal farm ought to be associated with an expansion of stock rearing on the hill farm.

Although ploughing out and reseeding is probably the most rapid method of pasture improvement, outstanding results have been obtained without resorting to the plough. The method here is to apply lime to the sward and heavily graze with hill cattle; after about two years a phosphoric fertilizer, usually basic slag, is applied and this is followed by broadcasting seed cleanings; by this method substantial improvement can be obtained at a relatively low cost. It is interesting that the first aerial application of lime and fertilizers took place in West Montgomery in 1950. Since the end of the Second World War, many difficult, inaccessible, and rocky fields have been reclaimed. Deep ploughing and bull-dozing have both been employed, and in some cases boulders have even been blasted so that reseeding could take place. In general, the farmers of Wales have greatly benefited from the Hill Farming and Livestock Rearing Schemes and from the Marginal Production and Small Farmer Schemes.

Emphasis has so far been placed on livestock farming, and it is certainly true that both climate and topography have combined to make this the dominant feature of Welsh agriculture. However, arable enterprises are of considerable importance in some localities. Thus mixed farming is of importance in Anglesey and early potatoes are grown on some of the better soils elsewhere, for example in Pembrokeshire and Flintshire; the latter two counties have the greatest percentage of area devoted to crops and fallow of any county in Wales (18·3 per cent and 16·5 per cent respectively as compared with an average of 9·2 per cent for the whole of Wales : the corresponding figure for England is 35·5 per cent). The south west of Wales is pre-eminently devoted to dairying and stock rearing; sheep are relatively unimportant. The better soils of the Vale of Glamorgan and the Plain of Gwent are areas of mixed farming.

THE PLAIN OF HEREFORD

It has already been mentioned that the Plain of Hereford is characterized by rich soils derived from Old Red Sandstone and overlying drifts. Here first-class permanent pasture is one of the most important features, and there are few mountain grazings. In addition, over 50 per cent of the land is under the plough and oats, roots, barley, and sugar beet are important. In the eastern part of Hereford hops are grown ; furthermore there are areas of fruit orchards, and cider production is important; the quantity of black currants has increased in recent years. But the area is famed for its livestock and the Hereford is not the only breed that has been developed here ; among the sheep, the Clun, the Kerry Hill, and the Radnor Forest types are native to this area. It is interesting that these are the only three pure breeds of British sheep that can be truly described as grassland ewes. Draft ewes are sold, traditionally at two years of age, at the autumn sheep sales. Farmers from all over the country attend the Clun sales at Craven Arms. Dairying is practised throughout the district except on the higher ground, which is devoted to stock rearing ; most of the dairy farms carry a sheep flock.

To the north and the south of the Plain of Hereford the farming is essentially similar to that of Wales.

CHAPTER 4

CENTRAL ENGLAND

THIS region is bounded to the west by Wales and the Welsh borders, to the north by the southern boundary of North West England and to the east by a line drawn in a southerly direction from Newark to Dunstable. The southern boundary runs north of the Chiltern Hills, through Abingdon, Swindon and Chippenham, then south of Bath to Bristol and finally north east along the Severn to the Welsh boundary. Thus the southern boundary runs for much of its course along the north faces of the Chiltern Hills and the White Horse Hills. The region therefore comprises part of Cheshire, South Derbyshire, South Nottinghamshire, part of East Shropshire, Staffordshire, Leicestershire, Rutland, most of Worcestershire, Warwickshire, Northamptonshire, East Gloucestershire, most of Oxfordshire, North Buckinghamshire, part of West Bedfordshire, North Berkshire and North Wiltshire. Included in the region are the following areas :

(a) The Midland Gap to the north west, and the Midland Plain.
(b) The Cannock Chase Plateau.
(c) Charnwood Forest.
(d) The Clent Hills.
(e) The Midland coalfields.
(f) The Northampton Uplands and the Cotswolds.
(g) The Vale of Trent.
(h) The Severn Valley.
(i) The Vale of Evesham.

GEOLOGY AND SOILS

The north and west of this region comprises the Midlands of England, an undulating plain mainly underlain by Keuper Marl and Sandstone, with outcrops of Bunter Pebble Beds and Bunter Sandstone giving rise to higher country such as the Cannock Chase Plateau. Charnwood Forest is underlain by Pre-Cambrian rocks. The Clent Hills are formed by a hard breccia at the top of the Coal Measure sequence. The various small coalfields of the Midlands give rise to industrial areas ; thus the North Staffordshire coalfield is associated with the Potteries, and the South Staffordshire coalfield is associated with the Black Country. Industrial areas also surround the Nottinghamshire coalfield north of the Vale of

J

Trent, the Ironbridge coalfield in East Shropshire and the Warwickshire or
Nuneaton coalfields. The density of population associated with these coalfields
mainly controls the choice of a farming system in the surrounding areas.

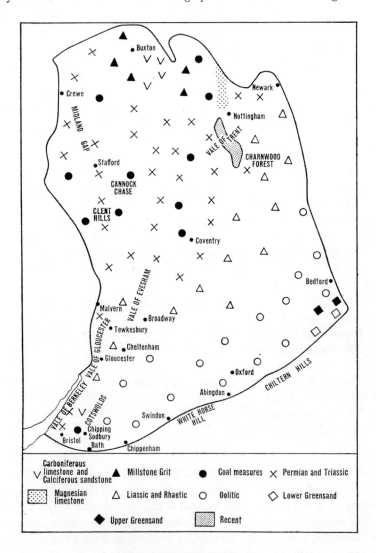

FIG. 19. Central England.

To the south east of the Midlands the Triassic rocks are succeeded by Liassic
and Rhaetic rocks and then by Oolitic rocks, both of the Jurassic system ;
thus the Jurassic system comprises two bands running north east to south west

across the region and gives rise to a succession of hills and valleys which often have a scarp slope to the north west and a long dip slope to the south east : such are the Northampton Uplands and the Cotswolds. Alluvial deposits are of importance in the Vale of Trent and, to a less extent, in the Severn Valley. The Vale of Evesham, on the other hand, is partly on Keuper and partly on Lias.

The soil types vary considerably over this region, and often light sands and heavy clays occur in close proximity—sometimes even in the same parish. In the north west heavy clay soils, with infertile sands on the higher slopes, are found, overlying Millstone Grit ; farther east, thinner soils overlie Carboniferous Limestone but these are often better drained and more fertile. The Keuper Marl gives rise to a red heavy clay soil with poor natural drainage ; such soils are typically non-acid and form some of the best of farming land, well able to withstand heavy arable cropping and giving high yields of many crops. Soils of this type are found extensively in the Midlands and in Cheshire. The associated Bunter series generally give light hungry sandy soils that are frequently acid. In many cases these are covered by gorse as, for example, in Sherwood Forest. The Bunter beds become very conspicuous in Staffordshire and Cheshire where again they yield very poor soils as in Cannock Chase ; this area is mainly open heath land though some of it is cultivated. However, some of the Cheshire soils formed from the Bunter support arable farming, especially where they have been marled. At one time the Keuper series was used for marling the Bunter soils, but this practice has largely died out owing to the heavy cost incurred. In general the Bunter and Keuper Sandstone coincide with low uplands whereas the Keuper Marls are associated with low ground.

The Lias usually gives rise to a heavy calcareous clay occupying lower land beneath the Oolite scarp. It is well developed in Worcester and Warwickshire and also occurs in Nottinghamshire, Leicestershire, Gloucestershire and Northamptonshire. The soils are generally low in phosphate and in some areas teart pastures are found, where grazing stock rapidly lose condition owing to the high level of molybdenum in the grass. On the whole, however, the soils yielded by the Lias must be described as fertile and there are few uncultivated areas on this formation. The Vale of Evesham lies mainly on Lias and here the soils, though not naturally rich, are productive as a result of intensive cultivation. Between the Cotswolds and the Bristol Channel running from Bristol and Chipping Sodbury in the south to Tewkesbury and Broadway in the north are the Vales of Berkeley and Gloucester, underlain by a variety of rocks including Lias, Keuper Marl, and Carboniferous Limestone. The prevailing soil type is Lias Clay but areas of very light sand are found around Tewkesbury and Cheltenham.

The Oolite Series is comprised of a number of divisions of sands and lime-stones, alternating with thick clay formations and giving rise to a succession of limestone hills and clay vales. The Inferior and Greater Oolites, known locally

J*

as white limestone, are typical of the bulk of the Cotswolds. The derived soils are reddish-brown and highly calcareous. Traditionally the area was devoted to sheep and barley, the soils being usually shallow and light. They are freely drained and are subject to drought.

Oxford and Kimmeridge Clays occur extensively in Bedfordshire, Oxfordshire, Berkshire, and Buckinghamshire. Both are calcareous, though the Oxford Clay is more so, and both give rise to heavy, cold, tenacious clays that are difficult to cultivate. In some cases, however, the limestone downwash into the valleys has a significant ameliorating effect and the resultant soils are of greater value.

Much of the region was glaciated and the soils are often of drift material; in some areas they bear little relationship to the underlying geological formation. The glacial deposits vary from light sands to heavy red clays. Some areas of chalky boulder clay give excellent arable land. The distribution of soils is further complicated by the occurrence of wide expanses of alluvium. Thus the clay vales are often modified by terraced oolitic river gravels. The calcareous gravels of the terraces and flood plains of the Thames are noteworthy; free working soils are formed from the alluvium associated with the Rivers Trent and Soar and also with the Severn.

CLIMATE

Meteorological data from four selected stations in this region are presented in Table 12. The low rainfall in the early spring allows the spring work on the farm to be started early and finished in good time. The lighter soils suffer from drought and on the Cotswolds the rainfall is typically 650–700 mm. Here the grazing season starts late and the winters are long and cold. Except in the west of the region the summer rainfall tends to be too low for high production from grassland, but over much of the lower lying ground the heavy nature of the soil is a compensating factor. Wheat grows well on these stronger soils, where the growing season starts towards the end of March or the beginning of April and lasts until early December; reasonable weather is usually experienced at harvest time.

There are three main types of farming in this region: one found surrounding the industrial areas of the north, another typical of the clay lands, and the third associated with the chalk lands. To the north the dominant enterprise is dairying, mainly as a result of the local demand for milk. The Keuper Marl supports good grassland, but even where the grazing period is short and much reliance has to be placed on purchased concentrates, the majority of farms have a dairy enterprise and many flying herds have been recently established.

CLAY LAND FARMING

On the clay soils, away from the influence of industrialization, in South Nottinghamshire and in Leicestershire, dairying has developed to some extent,

TABLE 12

SOME CLIMATIC DATA FOR CENTRAL ENGLAND

Station	J	F	M	A	M	J	J	A	S	O	N	D	Y
Total rainfall (mm)													
Nottingham	58	45	37	45	50	37	64	60	50	57	58	52	613
Coventry	63	45	41	51	55	44	66	65	56	62	66	58	672
Oxford	60	45	42	48	52	43	61	57	56	64	66	58	652
Malvern	75	52	49	55	65	46	66	68	61	72	73	68	750
Monthly mean temperature (°C)													
Nottingham	3·9	4·2	6·1	8·5	11·5	14·7	16·8	16·2	14·0	10·2	6·4	4·4	9·7
Coventry	3·6	3·9	5·9	8·3	11·4	14·7	16·7	16·1	13·8	9·9	6·1	4·1	9·5
Oxford	4·4	4·5	6·4	8·9	12·0	15·1	17·1	16·7	14·4	10·4	6·7	4·6	10·1
Malvern	4·1	4·3	6·4	8·8	11·8	15·0	16·8	16·5	14·1	10·3	6·6	4·7	10·0
Monthly mean earth temperature at 30·5 cm (°C)													
Nottingham	3·3	3·3	4·4	7·4	10·9	14·6	16·5	16·2	14·0	10·3	6·3	4·1	9·3
Coventry	4·2	4·2	5·4	8·4	11·9	15·6	17·3	16·8	14·8	11·1	7·4	5·1	10·2
Oxford	4·1	4·2	5·7	9·0	12·7	16·2	17·9	17·7	15·6	11·4	7·4	4·8	10·6
Malvern	3·7	3·6	5·1	8·4	11·9	15·6	17·4	16·9	14·8	10·8	7·0	4·6	10·0
Bright sunshine daily mean (hours)													
Nottingham	1·25	1·91	3·11	4·31	5·36	6·01	5·46	5·09	4·07	2·92	1·69	1·10	3·52
Coventry	1·13	1·96	3·23	4·53	5·41	6·04	5·36	5·25	4·15	2·93	1·55	0·94	3·54
Oxford	1·70	2·47	3·95	5·00	5·82	6·68	5·87	5·65	4·45	3·35	2·07	1·63	4·05
Malvern	1·86	2·54	3·97	5·12	6·08	6·92	6·04	5·80	4·64	3·38	2·13	1·73	4·18

but livestock production is mainly based on beef and, in particular, the summer fattening of beef stores ; the Lincoln Red or Shorthorn type is still popular, but today Friesian cross cattle are often predominant. In these areas sheep have also increased in popularity and here the Clun and the Kerry from the West Country are crossed with a Down tup for fat lamb production. Forward creep grazing has resulted in an intensification of the sheep enterprise. A similar picture is found farther south in Northamptonshire, though here there is a tendency for the farming to be more mixed ; many farmers are producing corn, milk and fat lambs, and many more have adopted a system of ley farming. A significant feature of the farms here is that since the Second World War the number of enterprises has been reduced from six or seven to three, or at the most four. Even on some of the Oxford Clay areas, where traditionally farming was based on the summer fattening of beef, dairy produce now accounts for 70 per cent or more of the farm incomes. In each of these cases the choice of a farming system has been dictated firstly by soil conditions which have led to a dependence on grassland farming, and secondly by the force of economic circumstances, which have demanded that the grassland be utilized by the more profitable enterprises of dairying and intensive sheep, rather than by the more traditional beef. On the alluvial soils cash root crops and barley have assumed chief importance, though dairy cows are again important on the leys.

CHALK LAND FARMING

As mentioned above, farming on the Cotswolds and other limestone soils in this region was traditionally barley and folded sheep carried on large farms. The large farms remain and, with mechanized corn growing being so profitable, barley is still the main crop, sown early to avoid the spring drought. But the folded sheep with their root crops have mainly gone as a result of the high labour demand of such a system. Dairy cows and short leys have assumed more importance. Sheep are still popular, and indeed have gained in numbers over the last few years, but they are now grassland ewes crossed with the Suffolk for fat lamb production. The economy of these areas pivots mainly on cereals and there has been an increasing tendency to reduce the ley break from three years or more to two or less. Here is an example of a system of farming resulting from the interplay of at least three factors—soil type, climate, and economic circumstances ; it is not possible to say that any one factor is more important than either of the other two.

THE VALE OF EVESHAM

One major horticultural area occurs in this region—the Vale of Evesham, though market gardening is found on the warm gravel terraces of the Severn Valley, around Bristol, and on the Triassic Sandstones of the north of

Worcestershire. Horticulture in the Vale of Evesham was noted by Arthur Laing as early as 1782, but the main impetus for its development came with the completion of the Gloucester–Birmingham railway (1842) and the Evesham–Worcester line (1852). No one factor can be considered as having controlled this development, though climate and topography may be most important with a rainfall of less than 635 mm per annum, a sheltered position, and the availability of frost-free slopes, particularly suited to fruit growing. The industry originated on the light loams of the river terraces which are well suited to horticulture, but has since spread to heavier and less suitable soils often derived from Lias. The nearness and accessibility of the markets of the industrial regions of the Midlands and South Wales has undoubtedly been an important factor in promoting horticulture, but it is noteworthy that the Vale of Evesham has, to some extent, a national market. About one-third of the area is devoted to fruit growing, one-third to market garden crops, and one-third to grass. Of special importance is asparagus, with almost a third of the total national output coming from this district.

CHAPTER 5

EASTERN ENGLAND

THIS region can be regarded as bounded to the north by North East and North West England, to the west by Central England, to the east by the coastline, and to the south by a line drawn from the mouth of the Blackwater River towards Dunstable. Included in this region are the East Riding of Yorkshire, North Nottinghamshire, Lincolnshire, North East Northamptonshire, Huntingdonshire, Cambridgeshire, Norfolk and Suffolk, the greater part of Bedfordshire, North East Hertfordshire, and North Essex. The region therefore comprises the following areas :

(a) The greater part of the Vale of York.
(b) The Yorkshire and Lincolnshire Wolds.
(c) Holderness and the Lincolnshire Marshes.
(d) Lincoln Heath.
(e) The Fens.
(f) The Breckland.
(g) The East Anglian Plateau.

GEOLOGY AND SOILS

Much of this region is covered by recent deposits : the Vale of York is a tract of glacial drift, lake silts, and alluvium. Holderness and the Lincolnshire Marshes are low lying and covered with deep boulder clay with patches of sand and gravel. The Fens are either dark-coloured mild peat soils or silts reclaimed from the Wash, with some islands of Boulder Clay ; the solid geology of the Fens is completely masked by these deposits. The Breckland is a large, mainly infertile tract of glacial coarse sands on the Norfolk–Suffolk border, which is now mainly devoted to forestry and has been largely planted up with conifers by the Forestry Commission.

Chalk is the underlying rock of the Yorkshire and Lincolnshire Wolds, of the western parts of Norfolk and Suffolk, of the southern part of Cambridgeshire and of that part of Hertfordshire included in this region. The eastern parts of Norfolk and Suffolk are underlain by Pliocene deposits and the part of Essex included in the region is underlain by Eocene and Oligocene deposits. Lincoln Heath is mainly underlain by Oolitic Limestone, which continues southwards through Huntingdonshire and Bedfordshire and is separated from the Chalk by a comparatively narrow band of the Greensand series of the cretaceous system.

The north west boundary of the region follows the west-facing scarp of the Magnesian Limestone series, and between the Magnesian Limestone and

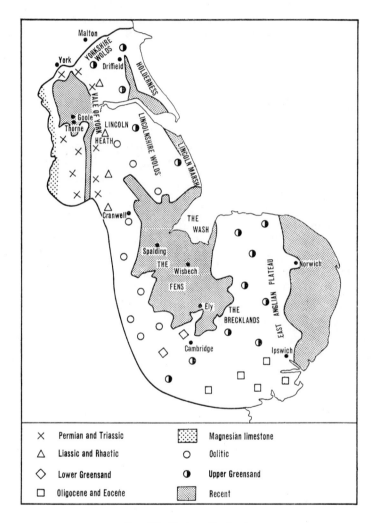

FIG. 20. Eastern England.

Lincoln Heath, south of the Vale of York, there occur Keuper Marl and Bunter Sandstone of the Triassic system and Lias of the Jurassic system.

The soils of the Vale of York have already been described when discussing the north east region and, because of the strong association between soil type and agricultural system, a further description will be left until the farming pattern is examined.

On the Yorkshire Wolds the soil is a light loam, flinty in places, and often free from glacial drift except on the lower part of the dip slope in the east where varying thicknesses of chalky Boulder Clay are found. In the Wold Valley between Malton and Driffield the soil is deeper and richer ; in contrast the top of the hills is almost bare chalk, and thin Rendzina soils are found. The Lincoln-shire Wolds are essentially similar with thin soils and often little or no subsoil.

Chalk also underlies the Plain of Holderness, but this has little influence on the character of the soil because of the deep Boulder Clay with which it is covered. Several distinct clays can be recognized, and these are overlain in patches by sand and gravel. The Boulder Clay forms a stiff rich marly soil, varying some-what in texture from place to place. The higher lying areas tend to have a more loamy soil and the lower lying areas a somewhat heavier soil ; this may be the result of water action carrying away the finer clay particles from the soil on high ground and depositing them in the sheltered areas. Similar soils are found on the Lincolnshire Marshes to the east of the Lincolnshire Wolds, though here the land tends to be somewhat wetter.

To the west of the Lincolnshire Wolds most of the low country is covered by chalky Boulder Clay which gives rise to the reasonably fertile, though often imperfectly drained, soils of Lincoln Heath. The surface is a dark grey-brown clay loam or clay with some stones overlying a yellow-brown clay with some mottling ; the chalk content increases with depth.

The deposits of the Fens are of three different types: (a) gravel, (b) marine silt, (c) peat. The gravels outcrop on the surface farthest inland and the silt on the seaward margin ; between these two is found the true peat. Most of the Fens are at or below sea level and the boundary of the Fen soils corresponds closely with the 20-foot contour. It should be noted that the Fenland is not in the main a delta deposit, since the mineral material has mainly been brought in from the sea. Fine silt was deposited in slack water and gradually built up until the growth of peat began ; the Fen peats are almost everywhere underlain by marine silt. Typically the soil profile consists of up to 900 mm of dark brown to black amorphous peat or peaty loam overlying a variable subsoil ; the peat is often calcareous. Following the drainage of the Fens, the upper peat has in many areas largely disappeared and the fen clay is now closer to the surface and within the soil profile. A feature of the Fens is the occurrence of roddons, which are the beds of former rivers now raised above ground level to form meandering ridges. The soils on these roddons are silts or silty loams, highly calcareous, and often showing mottling in the lower horizons ; the silt is micaceous. Such soils are essentially similar to the Fen silts of the coastal strip.

The area immediately to the west of the Fenland consists of variable calcareous loams and sandy loams developed on river gravel ; in some areas these are poorly drained and give Gley soils, in others they give Brown Earths. Associated with the natural Fen soils are the warp soils which have been formed by allowing silt-laden tidal waters to flow rapidly through sluices onto selected lands and then to drain slowly away. The silt alluvium is deposited and the resultant warp soils are of extraordinary fertility. The Humber is considered to be the richest in silt of all British rivers, and warp soils in this area are among the most fertile in the British Isles.

The majority of the Breckland soils may be classified as Brown Earths underlain by a glacial till consisting of a mixture of chalk and sand. The insoluble sand forms the parent material of the soil ; such soil is light in texture, excessively drained, and naturally acid. The A horizon is typically grey-brown and overlies a red-brown or brown B horizon immediately above the chalky till. Some of the Breckland soils have been improved by marling.

The East Anglian Plateau is largely covered by chalky Boulder Clay. The nature of the Boulder Clay is mainly determined by the underlying rock since much of the material has been transported only a short distance. The derived soil is essentially similar to that previously described for the Lincoln Heath. There are, however, other parent materials : thus the fertile soils near Norwich are formed from a Boulder Clay termed Cromer till—a heavy brown clay ; glacial or fluvioglacial gravels cover large areas of uncultivated land in Norfolk, in Suffolk, and in Cambridgeshire.

CLIMATE

The figures presented in Table 13 give some indication of the climate of this region. The rainfall is almost everywhere less than 635 mm, and one of the two driest areas of the British Isles (in Cambridgeshire) is included. Over the majority of the region the average daily bright sunshine falls between 4 and $4\frac{1}{2}$ hours as compared with about $3\frac{1}{2}$ hours for the north east. The climate in East Anglia is the most suited for wheat growing of any region in Great Britain ; but even here the atmosphere is too moist, and ripening is too slow, to give a strong bread wheat. However, much British wheat is used for biscuit making, and in the production of baking flour it is usual to blend the weaker home produced wheats with the stronger imported grain.

THE VALE OF YORK

The agricultural systems of the Vale of York were mentioned in connection with the north east of England. The area lies in the rain- and humidity-shadow east of the Pennines, and has a generally uniform climate with a low rainfall which nevertheless decreases slightly from 660 mm in the northern part previously described to 585 mm in the south. This difference is associated

TABLE 13

SOME CLIMATIC DATA FOR EASTERN ENGLAND

Station	J	F	M	A	M	J	J	A	S	O	N	D	Y
Total rainfall (mm)													
York	59	43	36	43	50	63	47	65	53	56	60	52	627
Cranwell	53	42	37	42	50	64	40	55	51	55	59	48	596
Cambridge	50	35	33	45	46	61	37	48	52	50	53	42	552
Norwich	60	46	39	47	43	66	44	53	59	64	68	60	649
Monthly mean temperature (°C)													
York	3·8	4·2	6·0	8·3	11·3	14·5	16·6	16·0	13·7	10·1	6·3	4·4	9·6
Cranwell	3·4	3·8	5·6	8·0	10·9	14·2	16·3	15·9	13·7	9·9	6·1	3·9	9·3
Cambridge	3·8	4·2	6·1	8·6	11·7	14·9	17·0	16·6	14·2	10·2	6·4	4·2	9·8
Norwich	3·7	4·1	6·1	8·5	11·8	14·8	17·1	16·7	14·5	10·5	6·5	4·1	9·9
Monthly mean earth temperature at 30·5 cm (°C)													
York	4·0	3·9	4·9	7·6	10·8	14·0	15·8	15·8	14·0	10·8	7·3	5·0	9·5
Cranwell	3·4	3·4	4·8	7·7	11·3	14·9	16·8	16·3	14·2	10·3	6·5	4·3	9·5
Cambridge	4·0	4·1	5·6	8·8	12·2	15·6	17·5	17·3	15·3	11·4	7·4	4·9	10·3
Norwich	3·1	3·1	4·5	7·8	11·3	15·1	16·6	16·4	14·2	10·3	6·4	4·0	9·4
Bright sunshine daily mean (hours)													
York	1·10	1·98	3·23	4·57	5·62	6·27	5·55	5·05	4·03	2·88	1·65	1·05	3·58
Cranwell	1·70	2·45	3·73	5·01	6·25	6·75	6·20	5·79	4·57	3·43	2·14	1·55	4·13
Cambridge	1·59	2·36	3·84	4·86	6·11	6·81	6·14	5·80	4·64	3·39	1·93	1·33	4·07
Norwich	1·67	2·41	4·17	5·18	6·72	6·84	6·58	6·09	4·90	3·55	1·92	1·50	4·29

with more intensive arable farming in the south and a greater dependence on mixed grass and arable farming in the north. The influence of industry is seen in the development of dairying in the proximity of the urban markets of the West Riding and the north east of England ; again the industrial areas supply the casual female labour required for the harvesting of peas in the south west. In other parts of the Vale the soil type has had an overriding influence on the farming systems. Thus on the peats and the warp soils in the southern part of the Vale around Thorne and Goole the farming is essentially similar to that of the Fenlands farther south, with sugar beet the major cash crop and with the development of numerous specialist horticultural enterprises including peas, brassicas and carrots. On the lacustrine clays, which are usually heavy and poorly drained, grassland is the dominant crop and this is utilized by beef, dairy, or rearing stock ; where such clays have been drained, farming is based on corn, particularly wheat, and on grass.

The Sandlands, partly of alluvial and partly of lake shore origin, mainly occur in the east and south of the Vale. Until about 150 years ago the heathlands of the sands were under their original vegetation. As a first step in reclamation, the soils were heavily marled with Keuper Marl, Lias Clay, or Lacustrine Clay. The objectives were to counteract acidity and, at the same time, to raise the clay content to above the critical figure of 3 per cent ; below this figure the sands are liable to wind erosion. Blowing or wind erosion is still a problem in isolated pockets where the marl does not come sufficiently close to the surface to make marling economical.

A feature of these soils is the high water table, and this is important in obtaining the high yields of cash crops often realized. For most of the growing season the water table is within the root range of crops and wide variations in summer rainfall consequently have little influence on crop yields. Such high water tables are largely the result of the underlying Keuper Marl and, whilst as indicated above, they are mainly beneficial to agriculture, they do impose some restrictions : drainage is always a problem and some deep-rooted crops such as lucerne grow poorly. The prosperity of these areas is largely dependent on sugar beet, cereals, and various horticultural enterprises.

THE YORKSHIRE AND LINCOLNSHIRE WOLDS

The farming pattern on the Yorkshire and Lincolnshire Wolds is mainly dictated by the soil and climatic conditions. The combination of mainly shallow light soils and frequent dry periods has led to most of the land being given over to arable cropping. Sheep are still important and in some areas they traditionally graze one-year leys in the summer and feed on turnips and swedes during the winter. Because of the uncertainty of summer rain there are few dairy herds. There is today, however, an increasing interest in intensive forms of beef

K

production, and many farmers are experimenting with systems of concentrate feeding from the calf stage, aiming at selling fat animals at less than a year old. As the potentialities of increasing the corn break have become realized, the system of barley beef production has become more common. An interesting feature of Wolds farming is the widespread belief that, despite the underlying chalk formation being often within 10 or 12 cm of the surface, lime should be applied at least once in the rotation ; experiments at the Ministry Experimental Husbandry farm at High Mowthorpe have, however, failed to demonstrate any visible or even measurable benefit from this practice.

HOLDERNESS, THE LINCOLNSHIRE MARSHES AND LINCOLNSHIRE HEATH

As could be expected from a study of the heavy nature of much of the soil, the chief products of Holderness are wheat, roots, and cattle ; on many farms the proportion under wheat exceeds one-third. Farther south in the Lincolnshire marshes it is more difficult to identify any one enterprise as being more important than the others. Areas of marshes occur which are used for grazing sheep and cattle and are often farmed in conjunction with nearby higher land ; such areas can be highly productive.

Nor is there an easily recognizable pattern of agriculture on the Lincolnshire Heath. Most of the land is farmed in large units of 200–400 hectares, and barley is the main crop. Sheep are of some importance and some roots are grown for folding off. In recent years there has been a move towards more intensive cereal cropping, and the area has lent itself to large scale mechanized farming.

FARMING IN THE FENS

The Fens are essentially an area of cash crop farming with very little livestock. The high fertility of the soils can be considered to be the main cause of the development of such a system. Both the silts and the fen soils are extremely fertile and their agricultural potential is enhanced by the flatness of the land. With much of the land being at or below sea level artificial drainage is almost always required : the field boundaries are generally open ditches and the absence of fences or hedges is a characteristic of the area.

The farms are typically small with over 70 per cent being less than 40 hectares. About 85 per cent of the land on the fen peats will be under arable cropping— half of this will be under roots (partly potatoes and partly sugar beet) and the other half will be cereals (mainly wheat). The small quantity of grass is mainly permanent pasture found on the small islands of Boulder Clay ; this may be hayed or used for carrying some cattle. Pigs and poultry are of less importance than is average for Great Britain though most farms have a small poultry flock. On the fen silts, cropping tends to be more diverse with 20 or even 30 per cent of the land being devoted to vegetables, the area devoted to cereals being reduced to 25 per cent. The area of permanent grass on the silt farms is often less than 10 per cent.

Thus the main crops of the Fenlands are wheat, potatoes, sugar beet, and vegetables ; most of the broad beans, celery, summer cauliflower, onions, and French beans that are grown in the Eastern Counties come from the Fens ; orchards and strawberries are concentrated around Wisbech ; daffodils, narcissi, and tulips are grown intensively round the Wash and in the Holland district ; bulb farms are centred on Spalding ; 70 per cent of the country's output of celery is produced in the Ely district ; chicory, parsnips, carrots, peas, flax, and herbage seed are also grown. The latter is particularly important because even this land benefits from a period under grass.

Highly fertile and intensively farmed though they are, the Fenlands are not without their problems. The need for artificial drainage has already been mentioned ; as a result of drainage and cultivation the peat is gradually wasting away, some of it at a rate of one inch depth per annum ; many of the culverts dug by former generations are now high and dry. No local building materials are available and, because of the shrinkage of the peat, building costs are high ; as a result farm buildings are few, often temporary, and frequently constructed of corrugated sheeting. The natural high fertility of these soils is, in some areas, becoming exhausted and farmers are having to use more fertilizer to maintain yields. Some of the land has been overcropped and the build up of diseases such as potato root eelworm and beet eelworm has become serious ; weeds such as couch and red shank are also a problem. Some of the peat blows very readily, destroying germinating seeds and filling up drainage dykes ; in a bad year crops may have to be drilled twice or even three times before a satisfactory take is obtained ; dragline excavators have been used for claying such land. Deficiencies of trace elements, particularly of copper and manganese, occur.

THE BRECKLANDS

Although much of the Brecklands have been planted up by the Forestry Commission, some of the land is devoted to agriculture. The majority of the topsoil has a high proportion of coarse sand and this overlies a chalky subsoil. It is the depth of the topsoil that controls the value of the land ; if the chalk is below 60 cm from the surface the soil is usually mainly coarse sand, extremely acid and deficient in potash; where the subsoil is between 45 and 60 cm from the surface, the topsoil is usually more of a loamy sand and more resistant to drought ; these are the soils that are cultivated. A common rotation is wheat, barley, roots, barley, barley, three-year ley ; the root crop is mainly sugar beet and the ley is often cocksfoot and lucerne, or cocksfoot and white clover. The land is more suited to barley than to wheat, but fair yields of wheat can be obtained immediately following the ley. Cocksfoot is chosen for the ley because of its deep-rooting habit which enables it to withstand drought; for the same reason lucerne is chosen provided that the land is not acid and that potash deficiencies have been corrected. The trace element most likely to be deficient is boron, but magnesium and copper deficiencies in sugar beet and barley have been identified. The key to continued cropping of these soils lies in the maintenance of a satisfactory level of organic matter; it is therefore important that all crop residues be ploughed in and that the ley is stocked as heavily as possible.

The utilization of the ley presents some difficulties: the lack of suitable buildings and the shortage of skilled cowmen have limited the expansion of dairying in this area; furthermore it is doubtful if the Eastern Counties can compete with the wetter areas of the west of England in the production of fat lambs; beef production is the remaining possibility and single-suckling herds have consequently become more popular as the importance of the ley break has become realized.

THE EAST ANGLIAN PLATEAU

The south east and the south of this region, including the East Anglian Plateau, can be considered together. Here, except for the area of the eastern part of the boundary between Norfolk and Suffolk where the soils are somewhat heavier and dairying is the main enterprise, barley and wheat are the main crops with barley predominating on the Suffolk and Cambridge farms. As detailed above, the soils vary considerably from chalks to heavy loams, but soil type has had less influence on the choice of a farming enterprise than climate. On the majority of farms well over 50 per cent of the land will be devoted to cereals and about 10 per cent to roots, mostly sugar beet, but with some potatoes— especially in North Essex. *Ley farming* is not practised to any considerable extent and much of the temporary grass is down for only one year. A common rotation is an extension of the original Norfolk four-course to five courses, with an increase in the cereal break. Livestock are not a prominent feature, and in some districts the farms are virtually stockless. Sheep here lost much of their former importance with the development of the fertilizer industry and the heavy imports of cheap lamb and mutton, though they still outnumber dairy cows by nine to one in South Cambridgeshire. By contrast, in Norfolk the rise in importance of the dairy cow has been one of the most striking developments of modern times. Beef production has retained some of its popularity. Mention must also be made of the expansion of the poultry industry in Norfolk and the prominent position of pig farming, especially in Suffolk.

Two other districts in this region must be mentioned: East Bedfordshire, where there is a marked concentration of " Cash Roots and Horticulture " farms, and North Huntingdonshire, west of the Great North Road, where farming is based mainly on wheat and cattle; here beef cattle are slightly more important than dairy cattle.

CHAPTER 6

SOUTH WEST ENGLAND

GEOLOGY AND SOILS

The south western region consists of Cornwall, Devonshire, and Somerset. To the west it is mainly underlain by rocks of older formations ranging from the Pre-Cambrian rocks of the Lizard through the Devonian rocks of most of Cornwall and of Exmoor, to the Carboniferous rocks of much of Devonshire and the Mendip Hills of North West Somerset. The younger Triassic, Jurassic, and Upper Greensand are found in the east and south east of the region. Granite masses underlie much of the higher land of Dartmoor and Bodmin Moor, where the derived soil is thin and mainly acid.

Except for some limited areas of alluvium the south west of England is almost free of drift material and the soils therefore bear a closer relationship to the underlying rock than in any area previously discussed. The soils of Exmoor are derived from Red Sandstone and Devonian Shale ; they are usually poor and, where cultivated, they need frequent applications of lime and fertilizer. Much of the land is open, unenclosed, and covered by gorse and heather. Traditionally the area has been devoted to livestock rearing, but in recent years milk production has assumed more importance, especially on the slopes of the hills. Much improvement has resulted from the Livestock Rearing Act and the hill cattle and sheep subsidies ; some farmers now fatten sheep where previously they were sold as stores. The major part of the cultivated land lies below 300 metres, though some land is cultivated up to 300 metres.

South of Exmoor, the Culm measures of the Carboniferous system are composed of sandstones and shales ; the sandstones give strong sandy soils and the shales give poor wet clays. Farther south still the Lower and Middle Devonian rocks have given rise to soils not naturally rich, but very much more fertile than the soil of Exmoor : the slaty members of the Devonian series weather to rather heavy clay soils and the grits to lighter soils. Volcanic rocks have given the most fertile soils of the area. In some districts, around Plymouth for example, limestone soils are found, and these also tend to be rather heavy and thin.

The Mendip Hills are mainly Carboniferous Limestone and this is quarried both for roads and as agricultural lime. The soils are some of the poorest in Somerset, and the area is bleak and desolate. At one time devoted to rearing store cattle and sheep, even here the dairy cow now assumes some importance,

135

and many of the pastures have been improved by ploughing, liming, and reseeding.

The Cheddar area is worthy of special mention. Lying in a bay formed by the Mendip Hills and thus sheltered from most winds, almost all of the land is used for market garden crops, and especially for strawberries. In the main the soil is well drained and of medium texture ; the slope of the land to the south,

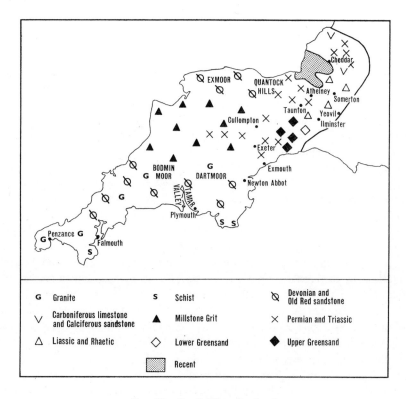

Fig. 21. South West England.

often considerable, allows the soil to warm up early in the spring. It is the combination of these factors together with the climate that has led to the development of specialist strawberry culture. Much of the land has been continuously cropped with strawberries over a number of years without any apparent ill effect ; alternative crops such as anemones, broad beans, and spring cabbage compare unfavourably in profitability with strawberries which, for heavy crops in a good season, will yield returns of over £2500 per hectare. The availability of labour for picking is the limiting factor of an expansion of the industry—many growers transport pickers over long distances.

The wide alluvial belt between the Mendip Hills and the Bristol Channel and the alluvial basin between the Mendip and the Quantock Hills have been won from the sea by a system of main drainage channels, pump stations, and low tide sluices, not unlike the Fenlands of eastern England. Some of the peat is dug for fuel, but most is used for agriculture. The main crop is grassland and the whole area is almost completely devoted to small dairy farms. At the southern tip of this area, around Athelney, 75 per cent of the country's requirement of basket willows is produced.

Farther east towards Yeovil and Somerton the land is somewhat higher and heavy soils derived mainly from Lias are found. Here again the emphasis is on dairy farming, though there are some sheep and some of the land is devoted to arable cropping. It is here that the Lias gives rise to teart pastures, owing to excess molybdenum in the soil. An interesting local industry is the growing of teazles, still used in the woollen industry in Yorkshire. Richer and more easily worked soils are found around Ilminster and again in the Vale of Taunton between the Quantock and Blackdown Hills. Here the soil is derived from Red Sandstone, and supports mixed farming and, in some areas, market gardening. On the Blackdown Hills, however, the soil is dominantly clay-with-flints, and the farms are small in size.

Many of the soils of this region may be classified as Brown Forest soils with varying degrees of gleying. The grànitic soils, however, are often well podzolized. From the above discussion it is clear that the special interest of the south western region mainly lies elsewhere than in the soils which, for the most part, are of indifferent value. It is true that in many instances flatness of the topography has allowed soils to be cultivated that would certainly have been left to rough grazing in a less kindly terrain ; but the dominant influence in the development of agriculture is the remarkable mildness of the winter. This is illustrated in Table 14.

CLIMATE OF THE SOUTH WEST

Over the major part of the region the soil temperature only rarely drops below 5·6°C—the minimum for growth of most agricultural crops; as a result grass can be relied on to give some growth almost throughout the year. It is this fact coupled with the rather high rainfall that has led to so much emphasis being placed on stock farming in the south west. The mildness of the winter also encourages crops to mature early and has led to the development of market gardening on land at one time devoted to mixed farming or dairying; such areas are found in the sheltered valleys around Penzance, Falmouth, and Plymouth, in a broad strip along the coast between Newton Abbot and Exmouth, around Exeter, and between Ilminster and Yeovil. Early flowers, such as

TABLE 14

SOME CLIMATIC DATA FOR THE SOUTH WESTERN REGION

Station	J	F	M	A	M	J	J	A	S	O	N	D	Y
Total rainfall (mm)													
Cullompton	106	73	63	61	61	52	69	76	76	90	109	105	941
Falmouth	132	95	81	66	66	50	71	77	78	117	132	134	1099
Monthly mean temperature (°C)													
Cullompton	4·9	5·1	6·8	9·1	12·1	15·2	16·8	16·4	14·2	14·0	7·1	5·2	10·6
Falmouth	4·6	4·3	5·1	6·3	8·6	11·3	13·1	13·2	11·8	9·4	6·6	4·9	8·3
Monthly mean earth temperature at 30.5 cm (°C)													
Cullompton	5·5	5·5	6·8	9·8	13·2	16·4	17·8	17·3	15·2	11·6	8·2	6·1	11·1
Falmouth	6·8	6·8	8·0	10·7	13·6	16·6	18·0	17·9	16·4	13·3	9·7	7·6	12·1
Bright sunshine daily mean (hours)													
Cullompton	1·63	2·51	3·97	5·46	6·07	6·98	5·87	5·76	4·62	3·33	2·06	1·50	4·15
Falmouth	1·88	2·63	4·26	5·94	6·83	7·67	6·42	6·31	5·08	3·60	2·45	1·78	4·57

anemones, and vegetables, especially broccoli, spring cabbage and early peas, are exported from these areas to other parts of the country. The trade of flowers for the London market is at its height between January and April. Orchards are an important feature of the region, especially in the coastal belt defined above, and along the coast of Somerset ; Devonshire cider is world famed and, together with Herefordshire, Somerset and Devon, are the main cider-producing counties of the country. The horticultural industry in the Tamar Valley was originally founded on fruit and has been noted for its early fruit since the middle of the nineteenth century ; immediately after the Second World War, flower growing was extremely profitable and many holdings in this fertile valley specialized in daffodils, anemones and irises ; but a slump in flower prices from about 1954 has resulted in added interest in strawberries and today this is one of the most important of crops. There is little doubt that the development of transportation has played a major role in the exploitation of the better soils of the south west.

LIVESTOCK PRODUCTION IN THE SOUTH WEST

Despite the economic importance of the horticultural enterprises, this region must be considered to be mainly devoted to livestock production. Cornish butter and Devonshire cream have long been famous and the importance of these products was largely the result of the relative inaccessibility of the peninsula. But the establishment of collecting stations for the direct supply of milk to factories has put more emphasis on whole milk sales. The importance of the dairy industry is reflected in the fact that this is the home of the South Devon dairy breed of cattle ; the importance of cream and milk products is emphasized by the high quality milk that this breed produces. It is worthy of note that the South Devon is the only breed of cattle originating in England whose milk qualifies for the quality premium, otherwise reserved for the Channel Island breeds.

Beef is also important and the North Devon is the local beef breed. Five British breeds of sheep originate in this region, thus emphasizing the importance of sheep farming on the poorer land of Exmoor, Dartmoor, and Bodmin Moor, where cultivation is restricted to the valleys and where most farms have grazing rights on the moor. Dartmoor is also famous as the home of the pony that bears its name, and the red deer of Exmoor must be mentioned. Of more importance, agriculturally, is the remarkably high population of pigs and poultry in the western half of Cornwall.

Other than horticulture, most of the arable cropping reflects the importance of the livestock industry and much of the land is devoted to the production of fodder crops. Certain of the drier tracts with more favourable soil conditions are producing limited quantities of cereals.

CHAPTER 7

CENTRAL SOUTHERN ENGLAND

THIS region is bounded to the west by South West England, to the north by Central England, and to the east by a line drawn approximately from Hertford to Hungerford and then south east to Eastbourne. The southern boundary is the coastline except that the Isle of Wight is included. The region therefore includes the Downlands of Dorset, Wiltshire, Berkshire, Buckinghamshire, Hertfordshire, Hampshire and West Sussex, together with the Hampshire Basin and the Isle of Wight.

GEOLOGY AND SOILS

The major part of the region consists of Downland underlain by Chalk of the Cretaceous system. To the north west of the Chalk is a belt of Upper Greensand and Gault, again of Cretaceous age ; in the west of the region is a belt of Jurassic Oolite. In the south the Hampshire Basin is underlain by Tertiary rocks and in the south east Greensand again borders the Chalk. The Isle of Wight may be divided into two areas with the northern half forming part of the Tertiary belt of the Hampshire Basin and the southern half being underlain by Chalk and Greensand.

The Chalk Downs form some of the most highly farmed soils in Great Britain. The most typical of all Chalk areas is probably the South Downs which are free from transported material and give rise to a characteristic landscape with many dry valleys and few running streams. Here the soil is often thin, red, flinty, and surprisingly short of lime. At other times, where there has been less cropping, the soil is pale grey and highly calcareous. In Wiltshire a true Rendzina consisting of 10 or 12 cm of black light free-working loam, often very flinty, overlying the chalk, forms the higher lying arable land. The lower parts of the valleys are generally covered with a heavier soil often devoted to water meadows—such soils are usually derived from Chalk Marl or Gault Clay ; soils on the slopes of the valleys are intermediate in type, usually deeper than those on the higher ground, but lighter in texture than the valleys.

In Dorset the Chalk soil is typically a yellow flinty loam, though on the higher ground around Winchester similar grey-brown light loams to those of Wiltshire are found. Strong thin loams and marls, with patches of red-brown heavier soils derived from clay-with-flint deposits, are found, for example, around Basingstoke.

At the foot of the South Downs the Upper Greensand forms a strip of land somewhat elevated from the Gault valley. The Gault weathers into a brown or light brown soil usually too heavy and too sticky for arable land and mainly under pasture ; where the Gault has been modified with sand from the higher

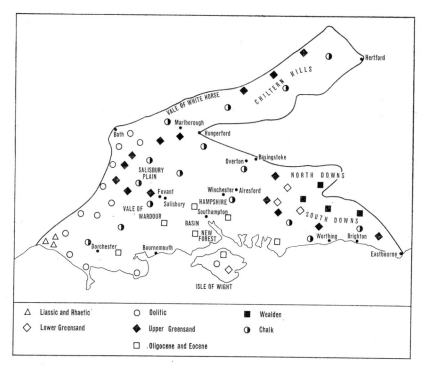

FIG. 22. Central Southern England.

ground, better soils result. In some of the Wiltshire valleys the Upper Greensand gives a fertile soil.

The soils of the Vale of the White Horse and the Vale of Wardour are derived from Kimmeridge Clay of the Upper Jurassic system, which together with Oxford Clay of the same system are found in areas of Berkshire and Dorset as well as Wiltshire. Under good management the derived soils will give good tilths, but they tend to be heavy, cold tenacious clays and expensive to work; an exception to this is where the limestone downwash from the hills is sufficiently extensive to have produced a significant ameliorating effect. Other Jurassic strata of importance in the west of this region are Cornbrash, Forest Marble, and Lias :

in particular the Marlstone of the Middle Lias forms some rich land in the clay vales of Dorset where the Forest Marble forms conspicuous escarpments. In both Dorset and Wiltshire the Corallian Limestone forms elevated ground, again with conspicuous escarpments.

Eocene strata of the Tertiary belt, in both the Hampshire Basin and the Isle of Wight, give rise to a variety of soils from heavy clays with impeded drainage to areas of acid gravel ; the Oligocene series gives a variable succession of sands, clays, and limestones. This series covers only a small area and is of little agricultural importance : the New Forest, for example, is largely unenclosed and mainly covered with heather and pine woods. In the southern part of the Isle of Wight, the Cretaceous rocks repeat the soil conditions already described.

To the north of the South Downs the scarp slope is mostly too steep for cultivation. Below the chalk lies a narrow ridge of Upper Greensand yielding a useful soil which carries some horticultural holdings. Beyond this is a belt of flat, heavy, Gault Clay mainly under permanent pasture. This belt is again narrow, and north of it stretch the ridges of the Lower Greensand. Sometimes the land is highly cultivated with some of the most fertile of soils in England. At other times, where the sand is coarser, some of the least fertile of soils are formed. These latter are well podzolized, white, bleached sands ; they are extremely acid, dry, and deficient in plant nutrients ; and they carry mainly heathland, common, or are planted with conifers. Such soils form the western heights of the Hampshire, Surrey and Sussex borders.

CLIMATE

The climate of this region is illustrated by the data in Table 15.

These figures illustrate the typical reduction in rainfall as one travels from the western to the eastern part of the country; thus Worthing has only 70 per cent of the rainfall of Dorchester. The monthly mean temperatures illustrate the general mildness of the winters; in the coastal area at least some growth of grass could be expected up to Christmas. Worthing, with a yearly daily average of bright sunshine of 5·03 hours, has one of the highest figures of any station in Great Britain.

DOWNLAND FARMING

Characteristically the Downland farm consists of two or three hundred hectares running in a comparatively narrow strip from the top of the Downs to the valley below and thus having a fair proportion of the different types of land found in these districts. Most of the valleys have two roads running through them—one on each side of the river; the farmhouse and the buildings are mainly on the roadside. Between the road and the river is found the heavier land—at one time typically devoted to water-meadows. Water-meadows are low-lying permanent pastures beside the river; by a complicated system of flood-hatches,

TABLE 15

SOME CLIMATIC DATA FOR THE CENTRAL SOUTHERN REGION

Station	J	F	M	A	M	J	J	A	S	O	N	D	Y
Total rainfall (mm)													
Worthing	75	51	44	45	42	39	54	58	55	75	87	74	699
Marlborough	87	64	54	63	59	50	73	69	70	87	91	88	855
Dorchester	104	73	67	61	60	47	74	77	84	105	120	110	982
Monthly mean temperature (°C)													
Worthing	4·9	4·9	6·6	8·9	12·0	15·1	17·0	17·0	15·2	11·6	7·9	5·4	10·5
Marlborough	3·6	3·9	5·6	7·8	10·9	14·0	15·8	15·3	13·1	9·9	5·9	4·0	9·2
Bournemouth	5·6	5·2	6·8	9·2	12·1	15·2	17·1	16·9	14·7	11·2	7·5	5·4	10·6
Monthly mean earth temperature at 30·5 cm (°C)													
Worthing	4·8	4·6	6·1	9·2	12·7	16·1	17·8	17·7	15·7	12·1	8·2	5·6	10·9
Marlborough	4·4	4·4	5·8	8·7	11·9	15·0	16·6	16·2	14·3	10·9	7·4	5·2	10·1
Bournemouth	5·2	5·0	5·9	8·8	12·0	15·2	17·1	17·1	15·5	12·3	8·7	6·2	10·8
Bright sunshine daily mean (hours)													
Worthing	2·17	2·93	4·74	6·05	7·49	8·11	7·49	7·05	5·64	4·02	2·54	2·03	5·02
Marlborough	1·41	2·26	3·89	5·23	6·01	6·67	6·14	5·93	4·79	3·18	1·79	1·40	4·06
Bournemouth	2·01	2·83	4·43	5·85	6·89	7·66	6·80	6·55	5·06	3·72	2·39	1·92	4·68

sluices, and drainage ditches these meadows were periodically irrigated by causing them to be flooded by the river. This drowning was carried out by the drowner who was considered to be a skilled craftsman. The aim was to flood the meadows over a period of about six weeks before Christmas and grazing could be expected to be available by March or even by late February. The water-meadows would again be drowned at intervals throughout the summer. But owing to the present high cost of labour, few farmers can afford to drown their land ; most of the fields are too heavy for satisfactory cultivation and in any case many are inaccessible to modern machines. Some of these meadows have been ploughed and reseeded, and some are now grazed by sheep, but others have been neglected and are now only moderately productive.

Running up from the water-meadows the land used to be mainly devoted to sheep with some arable near the road and on the flat top of the ridge. This was therefore originally sheep and barley land. Today, as a result of mechanization and modern fertilizer practices, most of this land is ploughed and the farming systems mainly revolve round grass and cereals. The grass is used principally by dairy cows, often milked in movable bails, though few herds are now out-wintered. The main cereal is barley, since it is best suited to this soil. Where the land is too poor or too steep for ploughing the chalk is typically covered by fescue, giving a short springy turf devoted to sheep. In some areas, Salisbury Plain is an example, the Chalk has a gravel covering and the pastures are rougher ; some of this land is used as a military training ground though some of it is still farmed, with dairy cows the main enterprise.

Two other aspects of Downland farming are of interest. Firstly, it is note-worthy that, whereas in most parts of the country the advent of mechanization led mainly to an intensification of the existing system, on the Downs mechaniza-tion, including the development of bail milking, led to a significant change in the emphasis placed on different enterprises. Land that was previously sheep walks was ploughed and now carries corn and leys : production from grassland was greatly increased and dairy cattle replaced sheep ; stocking rates were raised, with a consequent greater danger of poaching the land in the winter, and hence inwintering became more important and a greater emphasis was placed on silage.

The second additional point of interest is that the soil on top of the Downs is often black and peaty ; cereals have frequently yielded poorly in the past and at times failed completely ; at one time this was thought to be the result of the fungus *Ophiobolus* (causing Take-all), but more recently a deficiency of copper has been demonstrated, and spraying the crop with a copper compound in the spring has largely overcome the difficulty.

Away from the highly mechanized corn growing of the Downs, both the fields and the farms are smaller. The climate and soils still favour the growth of grass and the emphasis has for many years been firmly on milk production with cropping taking second place. Before transport became readily available, the milk was made into butter, using hand-skimmed cream; the skim milk was made into cheese and the whey was fed to pigs—hence the development of the bacon curing industries at Calne and at Swindon.

THE HAMPSHIRE BASIN

In the Hampshire Basin the considerable variations in soil type over relatively small distances are associated with considerable variations in farming systems. Furthermore, the choice of a farming system is often governed by the influence of urban development. Hence dairy farms, market gardens, and poultry farms are all found in close proximity one to another. Horticulture in this region is largely centred on Southampton and in the Botley district are found many hectares of early strawberries. Watercress is another product typical of Hampshire and this is centred at Alresford and Overton. Some emphasis on this crop is also found at Bowerchalke and Fovant in Wiltshire.

Horticulture has developed in parts of this region other than around Southampton. Thus many market gardens are found around Bournemouth, Worthing and Brighton. In some cases the soils are far from ideal for such intensive use, and the dominant influence in land utilization is undoubtedly urban development.

CHAPTER 8

SOUTH EAST ENGLAND

THIS region comprises the London Basin, the North Downs, and the Weald and therefore includes the counties of Surrey, Sussex, Kent, Middlesex, Buckinghamshire, part of Hertfordshire and the southern part of Essex.

GEOLOGY AND SOILS OF THE SOUTH EAST

The London Basin is a comparatively small, but nevertheless complex, area. It forms a triangular area from the eastern border of Wiltshire at Hungerford to Deal in Kent and north to Ipswich. The north east part of the Basin, north of a line between Hertford and the mouth of the Blackwater River, has already been considered (see Eastern England). The Basin is underlain by Eocene deposits, of which three subdivisions are recognized : London Clay, the Bagshot Sands, and Lower London Tertiaries ; the last subdivision includes the Blackheath and Oldhaven Beds, the Woolwich and Reading Beds, and the Thanet Sands.

South of the London Basin lie the North Downs with a similar succession of Cretaceous deposits to that described for the South Downs, though here the north to south succession is reversed and here also the Lower Greensand gives a more distinctive region. The Weald itself, lying between the North and South Downs, is underlain by the Wealden deposit of the Cretaceous system and there are two extensive alluvial deposits to consider—the Romney Marsh and the Pevensey Levels.

The London Clay is a blue plastic clay that weathers to brown at the surface. It is non-calcareous, difficult to drain, wet in winter, and dries out in the summer with consequent cracking. Much of this land holds grass well and areas of permanent pasture have been laid out in ridges and furrows to assist drainage. To the west and again in Sussex the clay becomes more sandy and easier to work. Generally the land requires lime and it also responds to liberal applications of phosphate.

The Bagshot Sands form the soil of the heathy barren country around Aldershot, Bagshot, Woking and Ascot. The soil is flinty and gravelly in character and in some areas, around Bagshot for example, it is almost pure sand. Where cropped, high farming is required with liberal applications of fertilizers and manures.

146

The Thanet Sands mainly consist of sands and flint gravels. Some areas of sands in the Isle of Thanet are highly fertile and grow excellent crops ; where the soil is somewhat heavier and more flinty it is usually less fertile. The Woolwich and Reading Beds consist partly of sands and partly of clays ; the clays predominate in the west and north. The sands and gravels of the Blackheath and Oldhaven Beds are virtually unimportant.

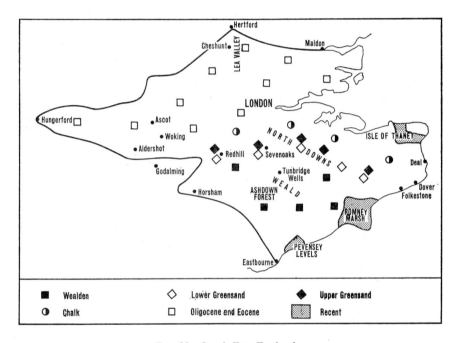

FIG. 23. South East England.

On the North Downs most of the Chalk is covered by clay-with-flints which gives rise to a variable mixture of flint and red clay or loam ; where free from this deposit the soils are essentially similar to those described for the South Downs. South of the North Downs, the Upper Greensand forms a rather heavy dark-coloured soil, which dries out to a grey colour. This soil is generally fertile and there is little waste land associated with it. Farther south still the Lower Greensand forms a strip of generally elevated country, which reaches a maximum width of about 19 km near Godalming. The derived soils vary from a heavy clay to a light loam. In Kent, around Sevenoaks, a free-working though rather stony loam, ideally suited to hops and fruit, is formed. In Surrey, west of Redhill, the soil is almost a pure sand and is mainly uncultivated common covered with heather, gorse, and conifers.

The Wealden series in Kent, Surrey and Sussex can be divided into two parts—the Hastings Sands and the Weald Clay. The Hastings Sands form elevated land in the centre of the Weald with sandy soils occupied by Ashdown Forest and tracts of heathland. Some of the sands are so fine that in practice they behave like clays ; mainly they are mottled below the surface with many iron concretions, in places forming a pan which must be broken up even to plant trees successfully. Such soil is always acid and often well podzolized. It is mainly in the floors of the valleys to the east that these soils are farmed ; here some hops are grown, but the main utilization is for grassland and dairying.

Much of the rest of the Weald is occupied by the Weald Clay, forming a flat plain of an exceptionally heavy soil, which is greasy, deficient in lime, and difficult to work ; such land is mainly devoted to pastures, though wheat, beans and mangolds all grow fairly well.

The Romney Marsh and the Pevensey Levels are two areas of alluvium which have been reclaimed from the sea and are in some ways comparable with the Fenlands. These alluvial soils include many differently textured soils in close proximity one to another and with an exceedingly complex distribution. The soil pattern is apparently related to micro-relief and to the way in which the Marshes were built up by tidal action. Thus raised areas form sandy ridges up to 200 m in width composed of light to medium textured soils about 45 cm in depth, overlying a calcareous fine sandy loam or loamy sand. The lower-lying areas have about 30 cm of clay loam or clay sometimes overlying a heavier textured subsoil which passes into a loam or fine sandy loam at variable depths, but generally below 60 cm; peat is often encountered 1·2 or 1·5 metres below the surface. Some low areas are occupied by poorly drained light-textured soils overlying peat. In other areas clay overlies sand at about 1 metre. The water table is also found to vary; in dry periods it may fall to below 2·5 metres, but in wet periods it will be at or close to the surface. In this area manganese deficiency in crops and copper deficiency in stock are real dangers; the practice of spraying crops with manganese sulphate is routine.

CLIMATE

Table 16 illustrates the climatic conditions of this region. In general, the climate is mild and not given to real extremes of heat or cold; nevertheless, the temperature range of London, for example, is 14°C from January to July, whereas in the south west at Falmouth it is only 8°C and in Eastern England at York it is 9°C. It is a useful reminder that the south eastern region has a climate most nearly approaching continental of any region in Great Britain. Much of the region is devoted to fruit farming and market gardening and the occurrence of frosts, particularly in the late spring, is consequently an important aspect of climate. In London thirteen days can be expected to have a ground

TABLE 16

SOME CLIMATIC DATA FOR THE SOUTH EASTERN REGION

Station	J	F	M	A	M	J	J	A	S	O	N	D	Y
Total rainfall (mm)													
Kew Observatory	54	39	37	46	46	62	44	57	50	57	63	52	607
Tunbridge Wells	77	57	50	57	53	58	44	61	56	83	92	80	768
Folkestone	77	52	46	54	50	65	44	61	64	89	97	79	778
Monthly mean temperature (°C)													
Kew Observatory	4·5	4·7	6·6	9·1	12·4	15·7	17·7	17·1	14·6	10·7	7·0	4·9	10·4
Tunbridge Wells	3·6	3·8	5·8	8·3	11·7	14·7	16·7	16·4	14·2	10·2	6·2	4·0	9·6
Dover	4·8	4·8	6·3	8·8	11·8	14·6	16·8	16·8	15·2	11·8	8·0	5·4	10·4
Monthly mean earth temperature at 30·5 cm (°C)													
Kew Observatory	4·2	4·2	5·6	8·8	12·4	16·0	17·8	17·4	15·2	11·3	7·4	5·0	10·4
Tunbridge Wells	3·7	3·7	5·2	8·5	13·0	16·5	18·2	17·7	15·3	11·0	6·8	4·5	10·3
Folkestone	7·9	7·3	7·4	8·8	10·7	13·3	15·2	16·2	16·0	14·3	11·7	9·2	11·5
Bright sunshine daily mean (hours)													
Kew Observatory	1·38	2·15	3·63	4·98	6·32	7·02	6·41	6·04	4·67	3·11	1·72	1·29	4·06
Tunbridge Wells	1·75	2·57	4·20	5·39	6·76	7·51	7·11	6·48	5·08	3·63	2·13	1·65	4·52
Folkestone	1·81	2·91	4·44	5·58	7·24	7·86	7·45	6·96	5·46	3·85	2·24	1·70	4·80

frost in April, four in May and one in June ; July and August are normally free from frost. This is by no means the most frost-free area of the country : the corresponding figures for Falmouth, for example, are five for April and none for May, June, July, or August. Rainfall within this region shows relatively large local variations mainly resulting from the elevated ground of the North Downs within the region and the South Downs to the south of the region.

FARMING IN THE SOUTH EAST OF ENGLAND

The dominant factor controlling the choice of a farming system is certainly the proximity of the urban community of London and its environs ; the intensive fattening of poultry in Sussex is an example of this influence. In many instances, however, the first choice resulting from such a consideration is, of necessity, modified by the limitations imposed by soil or by climate. The proximity of London has influenced the farming system in a rather interesting way ; Surrey has long been regarded as the home of the hobby farmer and there are certainly quite a large number of successful business men who travel to London each day and concentrate on farming in the evenings, at weekends, and during vacations. The holdings of these farmers often stand out because of the high investment in new buildings and other improvements—often higher than the natural fertility of the land would appear to warrant. The farms are usually devoted to the breeding and rearing of high performance pedigree cattle. Because of the demand for such farms, land prices are maintained at a higher level than similar land in other parts of the country.

As could be expected, much of the region is devoted to horticulture, especially along the southern margin of the London Basin in North Kent, and on the stretches of brick earth, terrace gravel, and river alluvium in the Thames Valley. Hop growing is perhaps of less consequence than formerly, and hop-picking machines are now replacing the Londoners who once relied on the hop harvest for their holidays with pay. In the Lea Valley is found a concentration of commercial glasshouses which is one of the oldest in the world and certainly the largest in Great Britain. Cheshunt, only 27 km from Charing Cross, is the centre of the industry. But the importance of the Lea Valley for horticulture is diminishing ; this is largely because of the pressure of urban expansion which has led to the demolition of glasshouses and the sale of land ; thus, outside the green belt, land values for housing or industrial development may reach £25,000 per hectare—a strong economic pressure for the horticulturist to sell wherever land use regulations permit. The future of the industry is consequently mainly dependent on whether or not the " green belt " boundaries are revised.

On the better soils in Kent are found most of the hop gardens and orchards of the region ; on the better soils elsewhere in this region, where horticulture has not developed, agriculture is mainly based on cash crops such as early potatoes, cauliflowers, broccoli and spring cabbage. A typical rotation in the Isle of Thanet, for example, would be early potatoes, mid-season and late broccoli, cauliflower, wheat or barley ; in many cases herbage seed production has become important as the restorative crop.

On the heavier soils of the Weald dairying and other livestock production are the dominant enterprises though even here (around Kirdford is an example) there is a considerable development of apple growing. It may be that the high cost of draining some of this heavier land can be recouped by a high return crop such as apples. The farming system is often influenced by the farm gate trade in eggs, cream, vegetables and poultry.

The Romney Marsh has the finest sheep pastures in the world, some of which fatten at least 35 sheep to the hectare. During the war much of this land was brought under the plough, but today the general tendency is for arable cropping as such to decline and reseeding has been widely practised. The Kent, or Romney Marsh, breed of sheep is ideally suited to the conditions in this area and the practice of outwintering them on the upland farms enables high summer stocking rates to be maintained. Management is aimed at the production of early fat lambs, and to this end the Kents are often crossed with a Down ram. In some instances the more prolific Cluns have replaced the Kents and these are mainly pure bred. The Pevensey Levels are similar in many ways to the Romney Marsh, but here the grassland is mainly utilized by cattle, largely because of a better supply of running water for drinking purposes.

It is interesting that in recent years many of these soils have been found to be as useful for intensive cropping as the Fenlands and there is an increasing trend towards growing vegetable crops. Similarly nursery work and glasshouses are becoming established and bulb growing has commenced. The possibility of potatoes, peas, cereals, and grass seeds, giving as high a return as fattening sheep, has now been recognized.

BIBLIOGRAPHY

ASHBY, A. W. and EVANS, J. L. *The Agriculture of Wales and Monmouthshire.* University of Wales (1944).

BEST, R. H., and COPPOCK, J. T. *The Changing Use of Land in Britain.* London (1962).

CENTRAL OFFICE OF INFORMATION. *Agriculture in Britain.* H.M.S.O. (1961).

GARRAD, G. H. *A Survey of the Agriculture of Kent.* R.A.S.E. (1954).

GYRTH JACKSON, B., BARNARD, C. S. and STURROCK, F. G. *The Pattern of Farming in the Eastern Counties.* Cambridge University (1963).

HIRSCH, G. P. and HUNT, K. E. *British Agriculture.* N.F.Y.F.C. (1957).

JESSE, J. H. B. *A Survey of the Agriculture of Sussex.* R.A.S.E. (1960).

MERCER, W. (ed.). *British Farming.* H.M.S.O. (1951).

MINISTRY OF AGRICULTURE, FISHERIES AND FOOD. *National Farm Survey of England and Wales.* H.M.S.O. (1946).

MINISTRY OF AGRICULTURE, FISHERIES AND FOOD. *Agriculture of the Sandlands.* H.M.S.O. (1954).

PAWSON, H. C. *A Survey of the Agriculture of Northumberland.* R.A.S.E. (1962).

RUSSELL, Sir E. J. *English Farming.* Collins (1941).

SANDERS, H. G. and ELEY, C. *Farms of Britain.* Crosby Lockwood (1946).

STREET, A. G. *Farming England.* Batsford (1937).

152

APPENDIX

INDEX OF WEATHER STATIONS (For notes to refs. 1-14 see page 154)

Station	Latitude	Longitude	Altitude (ft)	Altitude (m)	Page
Bellingham[1]	55° 13′	2° 18′ W.	849	259	91
Bodorgan (Llangadwaladr)	53° 11′	4° 25′ W.	120	37	116
Bournemouth[2]	50° 43′	1° 53′ W.	139	42	143
Britton Ferry (Cefn Cwrt)	51° 38′	3° 49′ W.	503	153	116
Cambridge (Botanic Gardens)[1,3]	52° 12′	0° 8′ E.	41	13	130
Cockle Park (Morpeth)	55° 13′	1° 41′ W.	325	99	110
Coventry (City Hospital)[1,3]	52° 23′	1° 31′ W.	241	73	123
Cranwell (Airfield)[1,3,4]	53° 2′	0° 30′ W.	204	62	130
Cullompton	50° 52′	3° 24′ W.	202	62	138
Dorchester (Waterworks)	50° 43′	2° 27′ W.	312	95	143
Dover	51° 08′	1° 19′ E.	19	6	149
Dumfries	55° 3′	3° 36′ W.	140	43	86
Dundee (Camperdown Works)	56° 28′	3° 0′ W.	300	91	79
Dundee (Mayfield)	56° 28′	2° 56′ W.	147	45	79
Durham (University Observatory)	54° 46′	1° 35′ W.	336	102	110
Dyce (Craibstone)[3,5]	57° 11′	2° 13′ W.	300	91	75
Edinburgh (Blackford Hill)[6]	55° 55′	3° 11′ W.	441	134	79
Eskdalemuir (Observatory)	55° 19′	3° 12′ W.	794	242	91
Falmouth (Observatory)[2]	50° 9′	5° 5′ W.	167	51	138
Folkestone[7]	51° 5′	1° 11′ E.	134	41	149
Galashiels (The Peel, Clovenfords)	55° 36′	2° 54′ W.	450	137	91
Girvan (Glendoune Gardens)[4]	55° 14′	4° 51′ W.	100	30	86
Gordon Castle (Fochabers)[8]	57° 37′	3° 5′ W.	104	32	79
Holyhead	53° 19′	4° 37′ W.	26	8	116
Hutton (Preston)	53° 44′	2° 45′ W.	82	25	105
Keswick (High Hill)[3]	54° 36′	3° 9′ W.	254	77	105
Kew Observatory	51° 28′	0° 19′ W.	18	5	149
Llanidloes (Mount Severn)[4]	52° 27′	3° 34′ W.	600	183	116
Malvern[2,3]	52° 8′	2° 18′ W.	380	116	123
Marlborough College[3]	51° 25′	1° 44′ W.	424	129	143
Newton Rigg[3,9]	54° 40′	2° 47′ W.	560	171	105
Norwich (Southwell Lodge)[10]	52° 37′	1° 17′ E.	110	34	130
Nottingham (The Castle)[11]	52° 57′	1° 9′ W.	192	59	123
Oxford (Radcliffe Observatory)	51° 46′	1° 16′ W.	208	63	123
Paisley (Coats Observatory)[12]	55° 51′	4° 26′ W.	106	32	83
Penrith (Hutton John)	54° 38′	2° 52′ W.	688	210	105
Rhayader[13]	52° 18′	3° 31′ W.	757	231	116
Ross-on-Wye	51° 55′	2° 35′ W.	223	68	116
Ruthwell	55° 0′	3° 26′ W.	67	20	86
Ruthwell (Comlongen Castle)	55° 0′	3° 27′ W.	95	29	86
Stirling (Sauchie House)[1,3]	56° 7′	3° 56′ W.	151	46	83
Swansea[1,2,3]	51° 37′	3° 55′ W.	32	10	116
Tunbridge Wells (Calcerley Park)	51° 8′	0° 16′ W.	351	107	149
Turnberry	55° 19′	4° 50′ W.	25	8	86
Wick Airport[1,4]	58° 27′	3° 5′ W.	119	36	75
Worthing[2]	50° 49′	0° 22′ W.	25	8	143
York[12,14]	53° 57′	1° 5′ W.	57	17	(110,) (130)

Notes: Unless otherwise stated, averages for rainfall are for the period 1916–50, and the averages for the other records are for the period 1921–50.
1. Records for temperature incomplete.
2. Averages of temperature from 1926 to 1950.
3. Records for bright sunshine incomplete.
4. Records for rainfall incomplete.
5. Averages for temperature from 1925 to 1950.
6. Values for soil temperature from Edinburgh University, with similar coordinates, but at an altitude of 69 metres.
7. Averages of bright sunshine are direct arithmetic means for the periods 1921–39 and 1947–50; altitude for soil temperature readings is 39 m; for rainfall records the coordinates are 56° 6′ and 1° 9′ E., with an altitude of 70 m.
8. Averages of bright sunshine are for the periods 1921–42 and 1945–50 ; records for a few months are missing.
9. Averages of temperatures are for the period 1921–47 ; a few months' records are missing.
10. Averages of temperatures and of bright sunshine are for the years 1921–47. Records of bright sunshine are incomplete. Values for rainfall are from the city cemetery, with coordinates 52° 38′ and 1° 16′ E., and an altitude of 28 m.
11. Averages for bright sunshine for the period 1925–50, with a few months missing.
12. The rays of the sun are obstructed during more than 5 per cent of the period when the sun is over three degrees above the horizon, for a few months of the year.
13. Records for temperatures and for bright sunshine are for the periods 1921–34 and 1936–50 ; the records for bright sunshine are incomplete.
14. The records for rainfall are from York Museum, with coordinates of 53° 58′ and 1° 5′ W. and with an altitude of 17 m.

TABLE 2
SOIL CHARACTERISTICS OF APPROPRIATE WEATHER STATIONS

Bournemouth :	Sandy loams above gravel.
Cambridge :	Sandy loam over gravel and chalk.
Coventry :	Loam.
Cranwell :	Loam over limestone.
Cullompton :	Light sandy, gravel drift.
Dumfries :	No information.
Dundee :	Loam and clay.
Dyce :	Light soil with a hard pan beneath.
Edinburgh :	No information.
Eskdalemuir :	Two feet of peat ; clay and soft rock below.
Falmouth :	Light sandy.
Folkestone :	Sandy top soil.
Hutton :	Clay loam and clay.
Keswick :	Alluvial deposit.
Kew Observatory	Loam.
Malvern :	Red marl and gravel.
Marlborough :	Loam over chalk.
Norwich :	Light sandy.
Nottingham :	Sandy soil on sand rock.
Oxford :	Loam and river gravel.
Paisley :	Dark garden loam over boulder clay.
Ross-on-Wye :	Sand over red sandstone.
Stirling :	Loam.
Swansea :	Sandy.
Tunbridge Wells :	Light sandy loam, gravel.
Worthing :	Loam and marl with clay in places.
York :	Sand over clay.

GLOSSARY

Cast ewes. At four, five or six years of age, breeding ewes of hill flocks are considered to be too old for the rigorous conditions of the hill. Such ewes will nevertheless be perfectly sound and are sold for breeding at lower altitudes ; these are *cast ewes.*

Concentrates. Usually refers to proprietary brands of feeding stuffs ; a more restricted definition is a feeding stuff or mixture of feeding stuffs containing less than 18 per cent of crude fibre (that portion of the feeding stuff insoluble in either hot dilute sulphuric acid or hot dilute sodium hydroxide). Feeding stuffs that contain more than 18 per cent crude fibre are termed roughages and these include hay, silage and straw.

Controlled environment. Modern intensive systems of pig and poultry production have led to the construction of special houses in which lighting, heating and ventilation are closely and sometimes automatically controlled— such houses are termed *controlled environment* houses. The advantages claimed for this system are better feed conversion, higher productivity and less incidence of disease.

Culled. Animals that are removed from herds or flocks because they are considered to be inferior for breeding or production are termed cull. Stock may be culled because they are too old or because they show some defect or because of low productivity. Culls from the dairy herd may be fattened for beef ; culls from hill flocks may be used for breeding at lower altitudes. The term cull implies purposeful selection.

Draft ewes. Ewes that have been selected for sale either as cast ewes or as cull are termed *draft ewes.*

Dual purpose. Dual purpose animals are those that are kept for two types of production. Thus the Dairy Shorthorn breed of cattle is termed dual purpose since after its productive life as a milk producer it can be readily fattened for the beef market ; furthermore, its calves can also be raised for beef.

Fixation. The term fixation is applied to soil nutrients in two senses. Thus phosphate fixation refers to the formation of phosphorus compounds of low availability to the plant ; on the other hand, nitrogen fixation refers to the formation of organic nitrogenous compounds from atmospheric nitrogen by, for example, the symbiotic nitrogen fixing bacteria ; the nitrogenous compounds are relatively available to the plant.

Flushed. To obtain a high lambing percentage, the ewes should be improving in condition at the time of mating. This is often achieved by grazing the ewes on poor pasture during the summer and then on good pasture for two or three weeks before tupping ; this system is termed flushing. In addition to giving a higher lambing percentage, a flock that has been flushed will generally lamb over a shorter period, thus making management easier.

Gimmer lambs. Female lambs are termed gimmer lambs or ewe lambs until they are shorn at about one year old. From this time until they have had a crop of lambs at two years old they are gimmers or shearling ewes.

Gleyed. Where a soil horizon is waterlogged and there is an accumulation of some organic matter, anaerobic conditions are maintained since any oxygen present is rapidly used up in the breakdown of the organic matter. Such a soil is termed reducing and leads to the production of reduced iron compounds, including ferrous sulphide ; these compounds give the soil a typical blue–grey colour. Where the water table fluctuates, aerobic conditions will be restored periodically, especially in patches of sandier material and along old root channels ; this leads to the formation of rust coloured ferric compounds in restricted zones and gives the mottled blue–grey and brown appearance typical of a gleyed horizon.

Hard pan. A hard pan is a continuous indurated layer in the soil that impedes drainage and the penetration of roots. Such a pan may be formed mechanically by the compression of implements resulting, for example, from ploughing at the same depth over a period of years ; a hard pan may also be formed chemically by the deposition of iron and manganese oxides and humates.

Heterosis. Crosses between different breeds of farm animals often result in offspring that show greater vigour than either parent. This hybrid vigour is expressed as stimulated growth and increased productivity.

Hirsels. An area of hill sheep land that will carry a flock of such a size that they can be shepherded by one man. The term hirsel is also applied to a natural division of a flock keeping to one tract of hill pasture.

Humates. Salts of humic acid formed from the decomposition of organic material.

In-bye. In-bye land is land that is in close proximity to the steading.

Leaching. Leaching is the removal of substances by the percolation of water.

Ley farming. A system of farming in which sequence of arable crops is broken by the inclusion of grass for a period of two to seven years.

Marl. To the agriculturist marl is a mixture of clay and calcium carbonate used as a source of lime and to improve the structure of light sandy soils. The marls of the geologist, such as Keuper Marl, are not necessarily calcareous.

Mor. Mor humus is strongly acid humus forming a distinct layer above the mineral soil as in a podzol.

Mull. A fertile mild or non-acid humus such as that derived from deciduous leaf litter, gradually merging into the mineral soil.

Poach. Soil that has lost its structure as a result of the trampling of stock or of being cultivated when it is too wet is said to be poached. Heavy clay soils poach more readily than light free-draining soils. A high lime and organic matter content also reduces the liability to poaching.

pH values. The degree of acidity or alkalinity is expressed by a pH value. The pH scale runs from 0 to 14. A value of 7 is neutral, values above 7 are alkaline and those below 7 are acid. This is a logarithmic scale and hence a value of 5 is ten times as acid as a value of 6. The pH value is in fact the negative logarithm of the hydrogen ion concentration. Most farm crops grow best at a soil pH of about 6·5 and will fail at a soil pH of below 4·5.

Shoddy. This is a waste material from the manufacture of woollens which is used in limited quantities as a fertilizer. Its value largely depends on its nitrogen content which may vary from 3 to 15 per cent.

Swards. An expression used to denote the vegetation of both permanent and temporary grassland.

Systemic insecticides. A chemical that is taken up by the plant through the leaf or the root system into the sap ; any insect sucking such sap is poisoned. Protection can last for several days or, in some cases, weeks. Systemic insecticides have also been developed for the protection of animals against insect pests such as the warble fly.

Tillage. Tillage land is arable land other than that devoted to rotation grasses, clover or lucerne.

Wether sheep. Wether lambs are castrated male lambs from the time of castration until they are about a year old. Between one and two years of age these sheep are termed wethers or wether tegs.

INDEX